Prayer Without Frills

Prayer Without Frills

by
Juan Arias

Translated by
Paul Barrett, O.F.M. Cap.

A PRIORITY EDITION

ABBEY PRESS
St. Meinrad, Indiana 47577
1974

The present work is a translation of *Preghiera nuda,* published by Cittadella Editrice, Assisi, Italy.

Scripture quotations are from the Revised Standard Version Bible Catholic Edition, copyright ©1966 and used by permission.

Nihil Obstat:

Fr. Cuthbert McCann, O.F.M. Cap.
Censor theol. deput.

Imprimi Potest:

Fr. Anthony Boran, O.F.M. Cap.
Min. Prov. Hib.

March 15, 1974

First published, 1974
©1974 St. Meinrad Archabbey, Inc.
Library of Congress Catalog Card Number: 74-83340
ISBN: 0-87029-037-1
Printed in the United States of America

Abbey Press
St. Meinrad, Indiana 47577

To all those who, in their fight for
personal freedom, have stopped
being afraid or ashamed
of letting others see them
as they really are

Table of Contents

Introduction

In the Bible, to pray also means "to cry out."
And we can cry out in anger, in pain or in joy.
In the Bible, man cries out, not to an impersonal taskmaster, but
to someone to whom he knows he can speak as a friend.
His is a cry that can never be without some element of love.
But for many modern Christians, praying means simply and
solely asking for something . . .
The poor man begging from the rich one;
The weak man entreating the powerful one;
The sick man appealing to the physician;
The savage wheedling the witch doctor.
For such people, God is not a personal friend with whom one
can rejoice and suffer, argue and get angry.
Their prayer is a self-interested one, the petition of an inferior to
a superior, a prayer that is hard to reconcile with the
revelation of the real dignity of man, who is called to sit
down at God's table because he has been given the power
to be equal to Him (Jn 10:34).
The present-day rejection of this type of prayer, which is more a
pagan prayer than a Christian one, more the product of fear
and need than of an awareness of man's dignity—this
rejection is not the result of atheism but is, instead, an
acknowledgment of the biblical God, who is no longer the

God of fear but the God who loved man unto death and
chose him as His friend and partner in creation.

Prayer Without Frills is meant to be a cry of rage and of joy at
one and the same time. It is not a cry of pride but of adult
and liberating love.

It is not insolence or impertinence, but the truest and most
genuine expression of one's naked conscience confronted
with the most authentic reality of oneself.

It is *prayer* because it expresses in words man's deepest needs
and feelings.

It is *without frills* because it does not follow any set patterns or
conventions, cultural or religious prejudices. It is simply the
real words of every human being who, face to face with the
reality of his existence, cries out without fear, without
shame and with all the power of his inalienable freedom
everything that, in the mystery of his own needs and
limitations, he feels is in contradiction to what others
impose on him.

Prayer Without Frills is not a literary work but is simply a
collection of the human prayers said in silence or cried
aloud which I have gathered here as the expression of a
humanity which is gradually discovering its own dignity
and its right to freedom and sincerity.

It is the prayer of the man who discovers that, if God exists, then
his prayer cannot be that of a slave who accepts his slavery
and can do nothing but beg for mercy and clemency.

It is the prayer of the man who discovers that praying does not
mean that he consents to be enslaved by anyone or for any
reason.

It is the prayer of the man who discovers that his God has given
him the right, not to beg as an alms, but to *demand* that
happiness which God, in a mystery of love, promised him
freely, asking only that he accept it.

These prayers were not composed in the quiet of a chapel but
sprang from the sincere experiences of actual men and

women with names and surnames; yet it seems to me that they express what many other people are saying as they walk the roads of our world, crying aloud, but perhaps without hope, to their God and their consciences.

The convict's prayer, for example, is composed of the very words of eighty prisoners with whom I spoke for several hours.

The parents' prayer is the expression of the thoughts of thousands of families who have come to me with their anxieties and doubts.

The young people's prayer was written after I had listened for years to the cry of a new generation which, in order to go on being Christian, imperiously demands the freedom to love and to feel that they, too, are persons.

The prayer of the desperate and the despised is my hard-won harvest of terribly painful human experiences, which matured me much more than all my university studies.

The woman's prayer is the cry and the suffering of that half of humanity which has not yet succeeded in making its own original contribution to history or in possessing its own personal identity card in the land of freedom revealed and offered by the Creator without distinction of race or sex.

The worker's prayer is the cry of the man who does not resign himself to being a machine because he, too, feels the urge to be a creator. Perhaps man's most tragic drama is that, although he has been called by God to fulfill and express himself in creative work, he frequently feels that he has been cast in the role of a slave, unable to come into the lordship of creation, a lordship that is already the foreshadowing and the reality of the joy of being "someone," capable of tasting his own happiness along with other men.

I have not made up any of these prayers. All I have done is lend my voice to cry out to other men what thousands of real persons would say to their fellows if they had the chance.

These prayers are the suffering, yet hopeful, cries of human beings who have not yet given up trying to be themselves, who are seeking a religion that defends every real freedom, who are seeking a God who is ashamed of, and rebels against, every abuse of one man by another.

These prayers without frills come from the wellsprings of human nature and will probably irritate quite a few of those powerful people of every class who try to take over from God by seizing possession of the most sacred rights of other men.

These prayers without frills will surely awaken only love—or disgust.

They will be hard to accept for those who are afraid to stand naked before the most fascinating and most demanding reality that all we humans carry within us. The believer will call that reality conscience; and the non-believer will call it fidelity to that mystery which continually cries aloud within us a word that is ever new, that is always truer, cleaner, more genuine and more impregnated with love than we ourselves are in the gray, alienating reality of our daily round, but which tells us what we really feel we are . . .

Because that reality of ours is more beautiful and greater than we ourselves are.

Consequently, praying means converting that reality into living words, into hope and human actuality.

The Despised

Today we come to you, Lord, we, the despised.
We are not a sorry procession, but a repugnant one.
We do not even arouse compassion or hatred, tenderness or
    sympathy.
We are simply despised; we disgust people.
The leper arouses compassion.
The fiercest criminal stirs up hatred or terror.
The mentally ill or the retarded inspire pity or protectiveness.
But there is no place reserved for us in the catalog of the works
    of mercy.

I, Lord, am a drug addict;
for all practical purposes, I have resigned from the human race;
I have lost all hope of regaining my self-control, of becoming
    myself again.
There are other people who have drugged, not their bodies, but
    their consciences and hearts.
But nobody despises them. At worst, they are feared.

I, Lord, am a homosexual.
I don't like women.
Now and then, I go with another man.
I commit fewer sins than my brother who certainly does like

women and who even takes up with other men's wives.

But no one at home or outside turns their nose up at him; they don't find him repugnant; on the contrary, sometimes they even admire him.

But everyone, both men and women, shy away from me.

And I am acceptable only to someone who, like me, also feels that he is cast off by normal society.

I, Lord, am a drunkard,

but a poor one.

I've been on the bottle for many years.

They don't want me at home because they're ashamed of me, and so I'm left to stagger around the streets like a sick dog.

When people see me coming, they hastily cross to the other side of the street.

Even a beggar occasionally has the consolation of having someone approach him and, although hurriedly, put a small coin in his hand, which, as you yourself have told us, is also your hand.

But nobody comes near me; except perhaps a policeman to hustle me off to jail.

Yet, Lord, there are others who also get drunk, but they do it at exclusive parties in the suburbs and, because they are influential, people only laugh good-naturedly at their drunken antics.

They are readily forgiven and, if necessary, excuses are found for them by their hangers-on, who cover up for them.

No policeman ever lays a finger on them.

I wonder—am I more repugnant when drunk than they are, just because I get loaded on cheap wine, while they do it on expensive whiskey, vodka and gin?

I, Lord, am a prostitute.

I can't claim to be one of the girls, not any more.

Because now I'm old and fat and tired.

I have no one now to pay the rent of an apartment for me and
   buy me nice things.
I am one of those who have to be satisfied with what the
   "customers" feel like giving them.
I no longer have a nice apartment to entertain my clients in, and
   I don't have the money to advertise in the newspapers as a
   "masseuse."
I have to be satisfied with hanging around cheap bars in the
   slums or on street-corners in the cold and the rain, hoping
   that some poor wretch will be willing to pay me a few coins
   for the remnants of my favors.
People passing in their cars look down their noses at me and
   quickly turn away so as not to meet my eyes.
I am despised even by the high-class call-girls who, glittering
   with jewels and wrapped in furs, glide by in big cars driven
   by their so-very-respectable "patrons."

I, Lord, have been excommunicated from your Church.
I can't receive the Sacraments, as do criminals and money-
   grubbers and oppressors of the poor.
Nobody even dreams that I may perhaps be at peace with my
   conscience.
Didn't the Church of your day excommunicate you?
There are others who defend more heresies than I; who even
   boast about their atheism; who exploit your Church and
   live off her without believing in her.
But they are admired and respected.
They don't carry the shameful mark of excommunication on
   their foreheads, as I do.
Perhaps this is because they have friends who stand up for them,
   or because they know how to be more diplomatic than I,
   professing in public what they betray in private or in the
   dark places of their consciences.

We and so many others whom society does not even pity; we, the

despised of the earth, who arouse neither hatred nor pity
nor fear, but only disgust, today we come to you, who are
sinless, because we believe that, if you do exist, you will not
despise but will even forgive us.

We aren't trying to hide or make excuses for the sins that have
caused us to be cast off by society.

We only hope that perhaps you, who not only forgive but also
excuse, will be able to avoid humiliating us further and to
tell us, as once you told the man possessed by the devil, that
saving us will let others see your glory and mercy in us.

Remember, you said you came to save what was lost.

And who is more lost than we who do not even arouse pity?

Sometimes a ray of hope lets us dream for a moment that
perhaps you may bring yourself to love even us and to find
under the filth and grime some traces of your own likeness.

Forgive us, Lord, if we are sometimes tempted to think that you
do not exist.

It's not easy to believe in you, whom we cannot see, when all
our fellowmen, whom we can see only too well, turn their
eyes away from us in disgust so as not to have to look at us.

Forgive us also if, as very seldom happens, we find someone who
does not despise us and even holds out a friendly hand to
us, so that we feel tempted to confuse him with you and
adore him as our God.

Forgive that idolatry.

But would it really be idolatry?

If someone succeeds in loving what everyone else despises,
doesn't he thereby become you yourself present and living
among us?

O Christ, have pity, at least you, our Lord and our
brother—have pity on us, the despised of the earth.

The Convict

Lord,
I am a convict.
I have more time for praying to you than do the Carthusian
monks.
But perhaps you alone know how hard it is for a convict to pray.
During every conscious moment of our lives, rebellion is
smouldering at the bottom of our hearts.
It's hard to pray, it's hard to believe, when you feel that you
have been abandoned by humanity.
It was hard for you, too, to pray on the cross, and you cried
aloud your anguish, your anger, your disillusionment, your
bitterness: "Why hast thou forsaken me?"
Perhaps this is the only prayer that we can say, but the world
just laughs at it.
Of course, your "Why?" was quite different from ours because
you were innocent.
We aren't innocent: but neither is any man on earth.
Yet our "Why?" is a plea for justice, although sometimes it is a
cry of anger, desperation and distrust.
We know that our "Why?" goes unheard by a society which
rejects man as a person and which listens to him only for
the sake of what he has or what he does.
Perhaps you still have a little patience, a little pity and even a

little faith in us, enough to listen to our anguished "Why?" without becoming irritated or sarcastic.

You, too, were a convict; you were accused, tortured and condemned.

One of the last things you did when you were dying on the cross was to give scandal to the professionally virtuous by canonizing a condemned thief without waiting for miracles or canonical processes.

To you, Lord, the living victim of all the injustices committed by human justice, we direct our cry.

Accept it as a prayer, although some "good" people may rend their garments at our "blasphemy."

Why, Lord, does society have to be inhuman with us, if it accepts you as the God of mercy and forgiveness?

You forgive and forget; you even find excuses for sinners.

But they, even when they forgive us, they don't forget our "moral leprosy."

We are marked men, branded as delinquents for the rest of our lives.

How can we hope to reform if society refuses to believe in us?

When I get out of jail, I probably won't be able to get a job, and I'll have to start stealing again if I want to eat.

And even if I do find a job, I will always be an "ex-convict."

If some of the people around me who have no criminal records pull off a job, suspicion will inevitably fall on me.

And then I'm well on the way to being sent up again.

But that's not all!

Why does suspicion have to fall on a convict's whole family, on his obviously innocent mother, wife and children?

They had nothing to do with his crimes, yet they, too, will be branded forever.

So, be very careful!

Society never forgives.

How can we go on believing in you, when your own Church
    can't do anything to erase the mark we carry on our
    foreheads?
We don't want to be pitied. We only want people to believe in
    us, to see that we can reform.
And we want to see them put their belief into action.
Lord, the brand that convicts bear is a terrible one, and even the
    innocent don't escape it.
Yes, some of us are really innocent, and perhaps the courts will
    one day recognize that fact. But even if the innocent
    convicts are cleared, who will cleanse them of the leprosy of
    having been in prison?
Society is crueller than justice itself.
Why, Lord, is it that the most defenseless people, the ones who
    are most crushed by the injustices of others, are usually the
    ones who are in jail, while the real criminals remain free?
Yesterday a black girl was brought into the women's jail.
She had shot a man who had got her pregnant after promising
    to marry her; then he deserted her, leaving her alone, in a
    foreign country and without a job; and then he went off to
    prey on other poor girls like her, unprotected and
    unemployed in a strange land.
Why wasn't he put in jail before the girl was driven to take
    justice into her own hands and shoot him?
And why isn't he and he alone in jail now?
And still, many who mete out this type of "justice" say that they
    receive you in Communion!
Do you understand now how our "Why?" is not absurd,
    although it is terribly bitter? They have taken away our
    freedom, but why must they so often take away also the
    possibility of making our time in jail an inducement to
    reform?
Why do we have to lose years and years, just staring at the grimy
    walls of our cells and the bitter, exhausted faces of our jail-
    mates?

If society still believes in us, why doesn't it prepare us for life
outside by teaching us useful skills and by showing a little
real humanity in the way they treat us?

But society has shown us by the harsh reality in which it
compels us to live, that when we do get out, we have no
hope of regaining personal dignity, really reforming and
taking our place once more in life.

That's why they sometimes treat us more like animals than like
people.

We no longer have any rights and whatever little we do get,
we're told that it's good enough for us, or that it's more
than we deserve, or that it's an unearned handout.

We're the scapegoats, and society gets rid of its guilt complexes
by hanging them around our necks.

Nevertheless, Lord, I wouldn't like to lose my human dignity
through having been in jail. I don't want to give up being a
person.

I want to believe that you, at least, the most just and most
innocent of all condemned men, are able to understand my
fears and my rage.

You alone are my last thread of real hope.

And perhaps this last ray of hope will make it possible for me to
pray for others as well as for myself.

Yes, Lord, have mercy on those who think that they are free
because of the mere fact that they have never been in the
hands of the police.

Have mercy on those who feel safe because they can steal
enough without running the risk of being put in jail.

Have mercy on those who have no criminal record but who find
it hard to sleep at night because their consciences keep
reminding them of the dirty deals they have been mixed up
in.

Have mercy on those who, in your name, in the name of the
Christ of freedom and justice, condemn us forever to the

greatest injustice by closing in our faces the doors to possible ways of reform.

Have mercy on me, too, Lord, when I look through the bars of my prison at a society that is a thousand times more criminal than me, with the result that I feel it impossible to confess my sins.

O Christ, let me believe in true freedom, that freedom which is within us and which no one can take away from us.

The Child

I am a child, Lord,
just one among so many millions of children all over the world
who laugh and play.

My name is not important; I didn't choose it; I was given it.

Don't ask me who I am, because I don't seem to have the right
to exist, since everyone is apparently down on me.

I'm always being told: "Don't do that!", "Do this!", "Children
should be seen and not heard!", "Don't annoy people!"

We children are never told: "You can!"; only: "You must!"

Parents say: "Wouldn't it be wonderful if they never grew up!",
but we think: "When can we be persons and think for
ourselves?"

Who is right, Lord?

Unlike the Apostles, you didn't find children annoying, so let
me speak to you, and then tell me who is right.

They tell me that one shouldn't lie, and then, when I let slip an
embarrassing truth, they get mad at me. Yesterday my
father got really angry with me because I said in front of his
friends that he hits my mother.

Is it worse to tell about something than to do it?

My father got angry when I told about it.

But I didn't dare get angry when he did it.

They tell me that it's not fitting to play with "certain children,"

and at bedtime they make me pray to the God who taught
   that we are all equal and that we are all brothers.
My mother tells me that I should be like my father, but my
   father steals, he phones the office to say he's sick when he
   simply doesn't want to go to work, and he's rude to the
   cleaning woman.
They tell me that children shouldn't think for themselves, have
   opinions of their own, or contradict people: because that's
   only for grown-ups!
But I can think for myself, I have my own likes and dislikes that
   are different from those of my parents, and sometimes I feel
   like shouting and protesting . . .
For example, when my father tells me to shut up only because
   he doesn't feel like talking, or when he tells me to go and
   play outside just because he wants to watch television in
   peace.
They tell me that I must not see certain things because I am a
   child.
But I think that only if I see these things now with the clean
   eyes of a child, then I shall be able to go on seeing them
   later without being ashamed as grown-ups are.
When they feel like it, they play with me as if I were a doll.
   Even if I don't want to play just then, they insist and, on
   top of that, they say that I'm spoiled and moody.
They are always the ones who decide when to play with me; but
   I can never choose my time to play with them. And when
   they refuse to play with me, I can't tell them that they are
   moody and spoiled . . . because I'm a child.
It's hard for us children to understand you, Lord.
You said that only he who becomes like a child will be your
   friend.
But all the people I know who say that they love you, who
   believe in you and pray to you—they not only don't want to
   be like children, but also prevent us from being so.
Yes, because they stop us from being spontaneous;

they make us tell lies;

they deny us the possibility of treating everyone as members of one big family;

they make us live like hypocrites and call it a good upbringing—

making us say what we do not think

and act like grown-ups,

like people who have "commitments."

Lord, I wonder who is right?

I remember that your parents once scolded you because you got lost. And you told them that you, too, had a life of your own and that you did not belong only to them.

Why don't you tell our parents and other grown-ups who deny us the right to be ourselves that neither do we belong to them alone, that what they like is not always the best thing, that we have a right to defend our originality.

Why don't you tell them that being a child is not a defect or a sin or a handicap and that a child is not just a pretty toy to play with; but that each child has a unique value, as you said yourself, a value that must not die in us but must be found always in us if we don't want to stop knowing you and loving you?

Do not, at least you, Lord, tell me to be quiet!

Listen to me and answer me!

And forgive me a sin that I've committed; sometimes I have the presumption to think that I am more grown-up than they are,

because I feel that I am freer: I can speak to anyone; I don't blush at anything; I trust everybody; and I'm quite happy to do nothing but watch the birds fly around.

I even like to eat dry bread.

The Student

Lord,
I am a student.

I'm very curious to know what you would do if you were a student today.

Whose side would you be on?

On the side of those who don't want to be bothered by anyone, who think that everything is all right and who only want to finish their studies as soon as possible so that they can get a job?

Or would you be on the side of those who are in no hurry to finish because they can't accept a world situation which is absurd even in the eyes of those responsible for it?

Lord, you remember that famous professor who was being heckled during a television debate by some student radicals and who finally got so angry that he burst out: "I know much better than you that our educational system is absurd and out of date. I'm not a fool!"?

And you recall what the students replied?

"The difference between us is that you accept the absurd situation and try to justify it because you are part of the system and you are afraid to lose your job, whereas we cannot in conscience take part in a set-up for which you people are responsible and which, nevertheless, you regard

19

as inhuman and outdated."

Whose side would you be on?

The professor's, or ours?

The side of those who would defend the professor, or that of the students who attacked him?

Because you weren't born to be a diplomat and were never afraid to take a definite stand,

We ask you to accept as our prayer the questions which nobody wants to answer for us.

Why do they compel us to waste a third of our lives in studying, not to gain real knowledge, but just to pass exams;

in studying, not what we'd like to know, but what society, for its own selfish interests, wants us to know;

not what would help us to know people better and communicate with them, but how to entrap and deceive them;

not what will be most useful for everyone, but what will earn each of us more money?

Why do they spend years teaching us what our ancestors did and said—and that wouldn't be too bad if they only taught us the truth—whereas they scarcely allow us a minute for creating something on our own account?

Why do they compel us always to think other people's thoughts although we often feel called to create some of our own?

A schoolgirl was told to memorize a poem by Wordsworth which she didn't like and didn't understand. Instead she recited a poem she had written herself.

The teacher reprimanded her and said indignantly: "That's not one of Wordsworth's poems!"

To which the girl replied: "I know it isn't. I wrote it myself. But I like it better than any of his!"

And she could have added: "If Wordsworth had been satisfied with memorizing other people's poems, he would never have written his own."

This schoolgirl was twelve years of age, just the age that you were when you amazed the teachers in the Temple at Jerusalem.

They were, however, less pharisaical and more human than the girl's teacher, and they marveled at your wisdom.

They condemned you only when you put your creative wisdom into practice, whereas we are punished the moment we do anything creative.

At least, you were recognized and listened to when you broke with tradition and gave your own interpretation of Scripture. People marveled at you because you said something new, something of your own, and weren't content merely to repeat what others had said. However, things are more complicated today.

Today there's more talk about freedom, but more locks are being put on all doors.

The result is that thinking for oneself is dangerous.

Creativity is no longer a godlike gift but a ticket to isolation, excommunication, exile, ostracism, hunger or the psychiatric ward.

People admired you, but we are despised at home and in school.

Sometimes there arises a great painter, a great musician, a great statesman, a great physician or a great poet who has no degrees or diplomas because he educated himself, and we say: "Of course, *he's* a genius!"

But we don't ask ourselves if perhaps he is a genius precisely because he has not been alienated by a school.

We do not ask ourselves if a man is a genius because he creates something different out of nothing, or if, on the contrary, we haven't got more geniuses because we don't allow them to fulfill themselves and develop their creative power to the full.

Wouldn't it be better to label as normal those who succeed in expressing what they are, and call those abnormal who are just rubber stamps of others and who never say an original word or have an original thought?

Lord,

We don't want to destroy the school or the university. We only want a school that won't destroy us, that won't crush originality, that will help us to discover and put into effect the dream that every man remembers when he awakens to life.

We want school to be for the man and not the man for the school.

We want the school of life recognized as the first and best school of all.

We want a school without degrees or examinations, teachers or pupils;

a school that is truly human and in which each person places his share of knowledge at the disposal of the others; a school where everyone creates together, just as they eat, play, rejoice and grieve together.

We want you to repeat to the world, and to your Church also, that no one should be called master or father.

You who were the only real teacher that history has ever seen were not a "doctor of the law." You were always simply yourself.

And that is why, without fear and without envy, you allow others to be themselves, too.

That is also why you told your disciples, simply and without regrets, that they would do greater things than you had done.

And that is why you were the real teacher of freedom.

Young People

Lord,
today more than ever before, we young people are searching for our
conscience.
We have begun to understand,
joyfully,
that our conscience does not impose on us a law that comes
from outside, but that you are present in the depths of our
being.
Now we know that nothing and no one can take the place of the
law that is written in our hearts.
We thank you, O Christ, because, although you are God, you
have not given us a law that goes
against what we are in ourselves,
against that thirst for justice that burns within us with the
diamond-bright flame of truth.
Unlike so many teachers,
so many false prophets,
you came only to help us to discover the reality of our
conscience,
to assure us of God's real presence in us,
to help us defend that presence.
You have given us the Church herself, not as a substitute for
your word that is written in us,

but to serve that word,
guarantee it,
and give us the strength to be faithful to it.
We accept nothing else as your Church.

We know now, Lord, that this discovery does not make our
journey to truth less arduous and more comfortable.
We must acknowledge that our conscience is more demanding,
more terribly just,
more devastating than any other law that could come solely
from outside.
We know that our conscience is truly above all law, because you
wish it to be so, and that this will sometimes lead inevitably
to conflicts since it is much easier to unload our
responsibilities onto others than to accept in solitude our
own obligations before you.
But at the same time, we feel happier,
because we discover that we are
more truly men,
more mature,
more ourselves,
more capable of searching for you with all our heart,
more painfully but more sincerely.
We feel the joy of true freedom,
that freedom to which you, the only true liberator, are
calling us.
Take from us, Lord, the fear of being free, and guide us towards
that freedom which obliges us to assume our responsibilities
to ourselves and to history,
not as robots or puppets,
but as real men,
capable of personal choice.
We know the joy of experiencing that, while conscience is God's
presence in us, the law is a pledge of love.
We young people are happy to discover, Lord, that not only is

love not a sin,
but that the only sin is not to love.

Lord, take from us the fear of loving,
because we do not wish to reject the strongest command of our conscience which asks us to love, and love always;
to love with that love which makes the one who receives it more free and the one who gives it richer.

Lord, we do not reject that love which we regard as a sin only when it stops being love,
that love which you are, the love which desires the eternal happiness of all men.

As we know, it is difficult to live and savor fully that love while we hear all around us the cry of the poverty, misery, and oppression of those who do not have the right or the joy of being able to love freely.

Lord, we feel that we are more truly members of your Church the more we seek together,
in the light of your revealing word,
and united around your table,
to form a common conscience among us.

If, Lord, you are *my* conscience, then you will also have to be *our* conscience because you cannot contradict yourself.

Therefore we feel that the only common language between men will have to be the language of our conscience.

Lord, we are confident that together we shall not confuse your voice in us with the unworthy subterfuges which our laziness suggests.

Help us, Lord, not to betray our conscience for any reason or in deference to any law.

Help us, too, loyally and peacefully to verify the authenticity of our conscience by comparing it with the conscience of our community,
because our assurance of possessing the truth is stronger,
the more it is supported by the loving, fraternal assistance

of our fellows.

Lord, may we young people have the courage to be ourselves, so
that you may be us.

Because only you have the words that we are looking for:
the words of truth,
those which speak unashamedly of love and liberty, words
which are there for everyone to use,
and which must not be denied to the oppressed, since we,
the heirs of freedom, cry out today against all slavery so that
everyone may possess freedom, too.

On Calvary you were love in chains; but we young people want
for all men the love of your Resurrection, that love which
has made all of us free.

Parents

Lord,
we are parents like so many others all over the world.
You know very well what our problem is and what we are
worried about—our children.
Like all other parents, we want the best for them.
But what we want for them is not always the same as what they
are looking for.
Perhaps never before have parents found themselves as puzzled
and at a loss as we.
Frankly, we don't know what to do.
Sometimes we're tempted to judge our children harshly and say:
"They don't know what they want! No one can understand
them! They're ungrateful and unthinking!"
We remember how we acted with our parents and we are
horrified by our children's different attitude: they haven't
even learned good manners.
Sometimes, when we are particularly discouraged, we feel
tempted to say that they are unnatural children.
Nevertheless, in our more optimistic moments, we can bring
ourselves to say that perhaps they are right and that we
haven't got the right to make them over into our own image
and likeness;
the image and likeness of a world, a society and a culture

that no longer exist or are disappearing.

Actually, they will be the parents of a society which we have never known,

one which is too new for us even to understand it. We feel that we have the right and the duty to impose our own tastes on our children because we still have the mentality of a society in which the idea of ownership and private property was pushed to an extreme, so that we say that they are *our* children.

Perhaps our anxiety and disappointment are all the keener because the change has been too rapid, almost brutal.

But then, even in the case of two brothers who are ten years apart in age, the difference in outlook is so great that they belong to two different worlds.

Lord, what are we to do, then?

You do realize that our situation is not an easy one and that it's no great help to be told that we should be more understanding.

Vague words of comfort are of little use to a drowning man, or to people like us who must stand helplessly by while our children pursue and embrace what we have rejected, feared and avoided all our lives.

It's not easy to regard as faith what we have always called atheism.

It is not easy to condone in the name of love what we were always told was sin.

It is not easy to regard as personality what we have always looked upon as impudence.

It is not easy to accept as a search for truth what yesterday we used to see as insecurity, lack of conviction and spinelessness.

It is not easy to esteem as respect for conscience what we used to condemn as plain disobedience.

It is not easy to honor as laudable nonconformity what we always took for sheer laziness.

And it is not easy especially to see it all at once and to feel and
suffer it in those who are flesh of our flesh.

Believe us, Lord, it is not easy for us to resist the temptation to
regard our children's attitudes as common ingratitude.

But although this may be our cross, deep within us we wish it
wasn't such a cross;
we'd much prefer to find that we are mistaken and that our
children are right, because we love them.

What is really torturing us is our doubt.

We are tempted to give them at least the benefits that we have
enjoyed ourselves, because we are afraid that they will not
succeed in getting even that far.

But if we were sure that their different and often opposite ideas
about the world, life, man and about our most cherished
values would make them better, happier, more authentic
and more devoted to truth,
then we and all other parents would gladly encourage our
children's newest enthusiasms . . .

Because we do love them.

Perhaps we don't know what it's like to break new, untrodden
trails that can satisfy the man who is not called to be a
fossil but an explorer.

Perhaps we have never experienced the bittersweet joy of a real
personal search, one which is both dangerous and deeply
satisfying.

Perhaps our middle-class income and our middle-class culture
have made us middle-class in spirit.

We have always thought that it is safer and less risky to sit at
home in comfort than go exploring.

But we seem to have forgotten that it is easier to become
paralyzed while sitting than while walking.

We have regarded everything new as dangerous.

We have thought that there is only one way to be truly human.

And because we are so security-minded, we tremble when we
see our children setting out along roads which we are

convinced will only lead them into a wilderness.

Perhaps our faith has been very far from real belief in the God
"who makes all things new."

And perhaps nobody ever told us that God is nearer to what is
new than to what is old, closer to what *is* than to what was.

It is quite possible, Lord, that we are paying the stiff price of
being middle-aged just at the time when a revolution has
struck the world with the suddenness and ferocity of a
hurricane.

We are the products of a world that used to exist and that
perhaps has seen its day, and now we find ourselves with
children who already belong by instinct, by necessity and by
history to a world that is coming and whose waves beat with
increasing frequency upon our shores, warning us of the
irreversible flood that is to follow.

Help us, Lord, to have faith.

Give us the strength to believe in our children's sincerity and to
accept the fact that they may be different from everything
that we have loved.

And let us not be so ingenuous as to think that a new world can
be built without failures,
without doubts,
without mistakes,
without weaknesses and without victims.

Look at our world, the world of yesterday, the one in which we
still have confidence! Wasn't it, too, built by men who had
to grope and stumble into the future?

It is imperative that we and our children now have:
sincerity with each other,
honesty in the search,
fidelity to conscience.

But here, too, we must make an act of faith in our children
because our ideas of sincerity and honesty may be quite
different from theirs.

However, Lord, no matter what happens, let us never stop really loving them,

but loving them for themselves and not simply because they are "ours."

In this way it will be easier to love them as they want to be loved and not as we would like to love them, which would be basically very like egoism and self-interest.

But, Lord, make them understand that our pain is real;

that our wounds are still open;

that we cannot help being worried, uneasy and perplexed about their future just because we do love them so much, but that this does not mean that we want to restrain their freedom to create.

Yet it does not mean either that they can indulge in hysterical ingratitude or forget that the pain which our love for them causes us is sacred even though it may be old-fashioned.

Grant us enough serenity to enable us to continue communicating with each other, at least at the most crucial and most trying moments, the times of greatest loneliness and misunderstanding.

May we all remember that if they are to be faithful to their conscience and if we are to have the courage to respect that conscience, we absolutely must go on loving each other . . .

because this love—increasingly more true, more unselfish and more purified, on our part and on theirs—is the only thing that will bring about the miracle of allowing them to create a new world without feeling that they are orphans and without having to be ashamed of us who brought them into the world.

The Atheist

I am an atheist.

This does not mean that I believe in nothing, but that I don't
believe in any Totality.

For me, God is a lovely dream or a beautiful poem.

I'm speaking now about a God whom I could love, because
there is another God,
the God of the despoilers of history, whom I would like to
murder with my own hands.

I am an atheist and therefore I cannot pray to anyone because I
do not believe in the existence of Someone who is different
from me and to whom I can pray.

Nevertheless, I have to confess that at times I feel very keenly
the anguish of utter solitude.

Sometimes I would like to be able to cry out to someone all my
thirst for I-know-not-what, and to ask him so many
questions that now have no answers.

But that would be like shouting into the wind.

Therefore I know that I must accept myself as I am, that I must
just plod along through the darkness of the world, that I
must not look for a definite answer to the problem of my
very existence.

It seems to me that people who believe in God are crazy,
although at times I catch myself wondering if I am not the

one who's crazy.

God, God, God!

Are you a beautiful invention of the poets?

Are you merely the echo of those who mistakenly think that they have found something to hope for?

Are you a cynical creation which the exploiters of mankind use as an alibi?

Are you the unconscious projection of man's need to be protected?

Of course, you could also be the one true reality that makes sense of men and things.

But what if you are only the product of a great illusion, of man's urge to divinize what is merely earthly?

Accordingly, I shall continue to shout my prayer into the wind.

I know that believers will laugh at me and say that this wind is really God.

But the only reality I accept is what I can see and touch. I accept man, who is always both an exploiter and the exploited at the same time.

Perhaps some are exploited only because the exploiters do not leave them with enough power to become exploiters themselves.

I accept also the mystery that I myself am, the fact that, on the one hand, I know that I cannot fulfill myself without other men, while, on the other hand, I feel the urge to grind them into the dust.

My God is struggle, revolution, justice and progress.

But perhaps He could also be something else: for example, a crust of bread eaten with my wife and children and which I earned without being a slave to the clock or to a factory whistle; a crust of bread eaten in a house without doors or locks, filled with sunshine, where a smile is not a luxury.

He could be the desire to be able to love at leisure, without the exhausting grind of an inhuman job that I did not choose

for myself and that numbs my mind, and with the certainty
that, if war no longer existed, the world would daily become
stronger, more creative, cleaner and more human.

He could be the opposite
   of the world's mad rush,
   of anger,
   of hatred,
   of vengeance,
   of oppression,
   of fear,
   of war,
   of neurosis,
   of pain,
   of sorrow,
   of death.

But then wouldn't He be a God for the privileged alone; a God
for escapists or for poets?

For me, God will begin to have a reason for existence, He will
possibly exist and may be worth searching for in a world in
which men can unashamedly use words which certainly are
natural to them but which actually have become
impregnated with the smell and taste and sound of those
who, by their everyday activities, prevent these words from
becoming the daily bread of all humanity and not the
privilege of a few . . .

words which are prostituted when they are used only by the
influential people of the world in the face of the anger of
those who, although they can say them, are unable to live
them . . .

words such as
peace,
freedom,
forgiveness,
love,
justice,

fraternity,
health,
life,
joy,
quiet,
poetry,
friends,
heaven,
children,
wife,
land,
man.

And "God," too.

Perhaps my God has a name which we men still do not have the right, or the power, or the possiblity and the desire to pronounce.

But when we can pronounce this name, perhaps my prayer will become possible and will be like rain on parched earth.

For the moment, however, all I can do is cry to you, the unknown and still undiscovered God, my uncertainty and the anger that wells up from the hearts of men enslaved.

The Man in the Street

I am the man in the street,
just another ordinary Christian, with no particular axe to grind.
Yesterday I was secure in my belief, but today the ground is
    moving under my feet.
Some people say that I am an atheist.
I wonder, however, if I have stopped believing or if, instead, I
    am really beginning to believe in a new way?
Only you know the answer to that, Lord.
I'm sure about one thing: I want to be wide awake, I want to be
    alive, and I don't want my faith to grow old.
I know that it would be easier to choose a side road and leave
    the main highway.
It would be easier to confine myself to defending what is old,
    closing my eyes to what is new, than to cut all the cables
    and launch desperately out to sea without looking back.
But would I be more a man if I did that?
I prefer, Lord, to travel as a pilgrim on the weary road of those
    who are seeking, without fear and without prejudice; of
    those who always fearlessly keep their doors open, and also
    of those who are not too proud to chew on a hard crust
    when they have nothing better to eat.
I am a man like all other men, Lord,
    a man who simply refuses to close his eyes to history.

And I hope that you will not condemn my daring in examining realistically the history of the past so that I can interpret the future.

I want to have the courage to admit that everything is not as clear and as certain and as definitive as many professional teachers of truth claim.

I can't forget, Lord, that all through history there have arisen false prophets who have stirred up the people with teachings that quickly withered and died.

I also know that not everything new carries your stamp of approval, but I know, too, that you are always growing, revealing yourself at every moment; that you are new every day and that you are continually calling me to follow you.

How can I forget, Lord, those who, in the past, suffered and underwent torture to defend what a Council of your Church has since approved?

How can I forget, Lord, that theologians whom your Church once fought and persecuted
      are today the ones charged with defending and promoting the orthodoxy of that same Church?

And they have not changed, Lord.

But today new prophets and new voices are being raised in favor of a step forward that makes many people tremble.

My Church fears these prophets, and fights and discredits them.

Yet how can I be sure, Lord, that these same people will not tomorrow be those who will judge our children's orthodoxy?

That they won't be the theologians of the next Council?

Don't you see, Lord, that it would be easier to close one's mind and defend only what is evident?

Yesterday I was taught to run away from those people who didn't share my faith, whereas today I am encouraged to enter into dialogue and fraternal cooperation with them.

Today we still call some people atheists,
      but is it possible that we shall discover tomorrow that they were more truly Christian than we?

Yesterday my parish priest, who left the priesthood for a woman,
used to walk through the streets of the town with his head
down, excommunicated and forbidden to receive the
Sacraments.

Today he goes to Communion with the rest of us and works and
smiles like everyone else.

Today my friend whose wife left him ten years ago cannot come
to Communion with us
because he has given to another woman, a woman who
loves him in return and takes tender care of his children,
the love which his wife spurned.

Is it possible that tomorrow I can be his best man when he
marries this woman in the Church?

Today they tell me that women must remain silent in church
and that my parish priest must be a celibate.

Is it possible that tomorrow your Church will give me a woman
as parish priest and ask me to confess my sins to a married
man with a family?

Don't you think, Lord, that it is better for my faith for me to go
along with my eyes open, not being frightened by anything,
accepting whatever comes, and concerned only with not
betraying my conscience?

Won't it be better if I continue pushing forward with other men,
unafraid of the unknown and not setting limits to your
revelation?

Won't it be better for me to take the risk of sometimes pursuing
a mirage rather than stop my painful but necessary
pilgrimage,
so that my faith will not die or become hardened,
and so that I will not betray those who are honestly seeking
in pain and hope?

Lord, I don't want to take my cowardice for faith.

Old People

Lord, I am an old man.

How far removed we are from biblical times, when being old
   was a blessing to be desired!

Today's technical, utilitarian world has made us old people
   superfluous, fit only for the scrap heap.

We're no longer productive, and therefore we're unimportant.

They grudgingly give us alms in the form of a pension so
   inadequate that they should be ashamed to offer it.

The world is so athirst for youth that our very presence is almost
   painful to it, like a bitter reminder of something that savors
   of defeat.

In a world in which everyone goes traveling, old people are
   particularly inconvenient because no one knows where to
   leave them.

Yet many parents can travel only because they can leave their
   children with the grandparents.

But when we old people are useless even for that, then there are
   the old people's homes, those open prisons, those graveyards
   for the living, those anterooms to the mortuary.

Lord, why is it especially the rich who feel the need to find "a
   decent place" to put their old people?

In poor homes, which are naturally smaller than rich ones and
   which cannot afford to hire domestic help, we old people

41

are treated better and are frequently loved and cherished.

Lord, few know what it means for an old person to be torn from his land, exiled from his mountains or his sea, and shut up in the concrete confines of a city which he had always avoided.

We are told that we'll be cared for better there.

But when we are not left to breathe our native air, we feel condemned to death.

Why don't they let us die where we have lived, loved and suffered?

At worst, would it be so difficult to build old people's homes outside the city, in our mountains or our meadows?

In that way we would at least be able to look out the windows of our prisons, or walk along the river where we fished as children, or pick the first ripe apple off the tree.

It's true that the pace of the world has quickened and that today we old people are forcibly reminded of our age because we are not caught up in the whirlwind of change that is sweeping through the world.

The concept of experience has certainly changed profoundly because in modern times a man can experience more in ten years than he previously could in forty.

It would be absurd for us to claim that we are full of wisdom simply because we are full of years.

Today even a beardless youth can teach us many things. It would be both unjust and ridiculous for us to claim that the world is much the same as it always was, when things have already changed so radically.

Perhaps, Lord, that is something we forget too often.

No doubt this has always been a temptation for older people, but today it is doubly dangerous because the world is on the brink of one of the most profound transformations in its long history.

Yet even if we accept this fact by acknowledging our limitations calmly and dispassionately and by confidently allowing history to search out new paths,

it still occurs to us to ask, Lord, whether we old people don't have something to give to the young.

We know that you understand us, although you never experienced what it is like to be old since they killed you while you were still a young man.

Perhaps this is why old people do not play a very big part in your Gospel.

We old people think that we have the right to say to the young, something that no one else can say.

We are not resigned to being thrown on the scrap heap as useless.

Today, perhaps for the first time in history, the young have discovered that their age group is not one of transition or of waiting, but that, as young people, they possess their own reality and wealth, which no other group has, and that therefore they have something unique, distinct and complete to say to history.

Since this is so, wouldn't it only be right to admit that old age is not merely a time of waiting,

of drawing a pension,

of gradual decline,

but rather a season of life with its own characteristics and qualities and with something to say to mankind that no other age group can say?

Perhaps this special contribution of old age has still to be discovered, and it is increasingly more urgent to do so nowadays, when science and medicine are so rapidly lengthening the average man's life span.

If mankind cannot discover the special message which we old people have to offer to the world, they may feel the diabolical temptation to fall into the worst of crimes, that of eliminating, no doubt very gently, all of us who, because of our age, are no longer useful to a swiftly moving, consumer society.

We think, Lord, that old age, accepted with serenity,
    without foolish pining for the past,
    without losing the savor of the soil and basic realities,
    able to look at the world with eyes that are beginning to see
    that, behind every thing or within it, there lies not only
    what it's worth or what it represents, but above all, what it
    is and what it's *for*—
    we believe such an old age can undoubtedly offer its own
    words of hope and wisdom to those who can see only the
    surface appearance of things, and who cannot even ask
    themselves why things exist.
An old person who is slowly and uncomplainingly sinking under
    the weight of the years, like the flame in a lamp when the
    oil is very low, can help others to rid themselves of the
    nightmarish fear of death;
    to discover the concept of time;
    to understand better that death is not the final, desperate
    farewell to everything that one loves, but rather just one
    further stage in the same continuous life,
    just as one goes from childhood to youth, or from youth to
    maturity.
A world without children would be a dull, sad world; while a
    world without old people would be one with many more
    suicides and insane asylums.
An old person can remind us at every moment that we can talk
    to a flower and not feel so alone;
    that water is good and beautiful because it is water;
    that there is a sort of time that clocks cannot measure, a
    time which does not end and which cannot die, that joy can
    have many names,
    and above all that love is not the fruit of only one season, or
    the privilege of only one age group, but a universal wealth
    that is more lasting than all ages and stronger than death
    itself.
Perhaps, Lord, if young people saw that we older ones loved

each other serenely, truly and with an uncritical love, and if
they saw us walking hand-in-hand through the streets and
parks,
their love for each other would be truer, deeper and freer of
tensions and anxieties.

If we old people loved each other more, it would be easier for us
to understand the idiocies of young love.

But how can we do that if society, by one of its greatest cruelties,
separates us from each other precisely when our love is
most mature and rewarding?

Lord, who will denounce this sin of society?

Can it be true that society doesn't have the money to allow us to
live together as man and wife at the close of our lives,
although it may only be in the same comfortable jail, when
money is never lacking to enable men to go on killing and
alienating each other?

You young people who are beginning to discover the sweetness
of love, won't you at least raise a cry in the streets and
marketplaces about this need of ours for justice?

Remember, Lord, that this is a problem for millions of old
people all over the world.

Remember, too, that old age does not take away our right to love
and companionship.

Our Lady

Son,
many people invoke my name and pray to me.
But there are few who believe that I, too, pray continually; since
I am not outside the history of men but go on living with
them.
I don't live in a happy nirvana, remote from men's pain and
untouched by it.
I am not a fairytale queen receiving nothing but adulation.
I am still living out my role in history and my tragedy as mother
of all men.
People go on calling me blessed, that is, happy, but I am
constantly aware that they are not.
Therefore, I must pray to you, speak to you, cry out to you;
I must urge you to advance the hour of liberation.
And I want men to know what I am saying to you, my son and
my God, my God who is also man.
That is the reason why I want to pray to you aloud. I want
everyone, both those who invoke me and those who ignore
me, to listen to me.
Too much stress has been laid on my happiness and my
privileges.
It's time that people knew more about my burden of sorrow; it's
time they realized that I am still suffering. I'm suffering

because my human role in the Church has been obscured.
They have made me inaccessible.

Instead of my being a joyful example for everyone, they have
made me a complete exception and an excuse for not
acknowledging the fact that everyone can attain personal
fulfillment.

Everyone can achieve what I have achieved, because everyone
can say a creative "Yes" that is capable of divinizing him
and creating a dynamic process in history.

I am not a kind of unattainable, untouchable "luxury" in the
Church.

Instead, I am an occasion of hope for everyone because they are
all capable of conceiving and begetting a life that will not
die.

I have given you to the world.

I conceived you with my "Yes," and by being faithful to my
conscience.

You are the fruit of my womb.

I was able to bring you into the world because I believed in your
word, which I received and accepted in the deepest recesses
of my being.

You were truly the first fruits of history.

Therefore, the real maturity and liberation of the world have
already begun and will go on.

But, although I know that this is so and although I see that you
have other gifts to bestow on mankind, I cannot be content
with that.

I yearn to see those gifts bestowed on men.

I shall go on feeling the pains of childbirth until the last man
feels reborn and alive.

My joy at having borne you and having brought you into the
world will always be accompanied by a profound anguish
as I wait impatiently and in pain for the birth of the rest of
mankind.

My joy will not be total and definitive until the last man has been born of my womb, as you were.

But, as you see, the birth of each man is a slow process, and few
are really born every day.

I feel a tremendous weight of pain within me.

Men are not born again because they do not succeed in being
free;

they do not succeed in making their own contribution to
history by being faithful to what is best and most original in
them;

because, instead of fulfilling themselves by listening to you
within them, they allow themselves to be deceived by the
empty words of those who do not believe in life and who
themselves are dead:

and because they insist on saying "Yes!" when they ought
to say "No!", and the other way around.

Hence it is difficult for men to see me as an example of hope.

My "Yes!" was hard to say, but it did give me the only real
happiness,

that of being myself and of total fidelity.

More than once the Church herself has been afraid of
emphasizing the reality of my "Yes!" to your designs in my
life.

When I said "Yes!" to being with child of the Holy Spirit, I
consented to appear as an "adulteress" in the eyes of men.

That's what my intended husband thought I was, and that's why
he was going to leave me.

Later you did remedy things, but at the moment of consenting to
be your mother, I accepted all the consequences.

I accepted the will of God which could have meant com-
promising my honour in the eyes of history.

I am regarded especially as the woman who "knows not man,"
as "the virgin," as the image of the most exquisite physical
purity.

But, actually, my glory and my greatest happiness come precisely from my being a mother.

I am the mother of God because of the demands of a total and
universal love.

In order to be faithful to the demands of my love, to follow my
only path to fulfillment, and to respond sincerely to the
voice of my conscience, I defied the laws of my time.

I trusted in your word, which was absurd to those who do not
know love and its very unexpected demands.

Although I was conceived without sin,

I lived a completely human life,

with all its sorrows and joys, anxieties and hopes,
temptations and perplexities, disappointments and victories.

I was betrothed; I was a wife; I was a mother and had the
joy of nursing you at my bosom.

I never renounced love.

But it was my "Yes!", my fidelity to my chosen role, that made
me free and therefore a "revolutionary."

Consequently, the awful wrench of your death was not the only
pain I felt,

for you were dying as soon as you had been born, just as a
fully ripened fruit has already begun to die.

And I continue to feel the pain of those who die

without having reached fulfillment,

without having been themselves,

without having been truly born.

I suffer when I see the injustice of those who allow their fellow
men to live and die without giving them the chance to
make their own particular contribution to history.

And this pain goes on.

Therefore, my revolutionary song:

"He who is mighty . . . has shown strength with his arm, he
has scattered the proud in the imagination of their hearts,
he has put down the mighty from their thrones, and exalted
those of low degree;

he has filled the hungry with good things, and the rich he

has sent empty away,"
which has so often been watered down by the Church, is
still very much to the point,
because the influential people and the tyrants of all kinds
continue to deny to the weak and simple of the earth the
possibility of existing and fulfilling themselves as persons.
Therefore my prayer is the same today as it was then:
"Put down the tyrants of history from their thrones and rescue
the lowly."
As for the self-satisfied, those who do not accept the pain of
bringing others to full birth—leave them sterile and with
empty wombs!
Hasten the liberation of all men, and listen to the anguished cry
of those who wish to be born,
who ask for the right to be men,
to have a history of their own,
which is being denied them by those who have taken
possession of history.
Hasten the time of my universal delivery, because only then
shall I be able, without pain and without shame, to hear
men call me mother.

Yes, I am not content to have only you as my child.
I need to see the smile of freedom on the faces of all those who
live in you.
Let them be born!
It is not enough for me to be called happy by those who admire
me or who pray to me as to a fetish,
but who don't believe that they, too, can come to share in
my life,
that they, too, are able to say "Yes!" to you.
I cannot bear to be unknown,
unacknowledged,
unneeded,
unsought,

and unloved
precisely by those whose lives are most like mine, who daily
cry out, as I do, their revolutionary chant, which is a song
of painful hope in the liberation of man.
I know that it is these very people who will one day understand
better than many who "worship" me today
what has been my greatest joy,
my keenest sorrow,
my biggest victory.
But I cannot wait any longer;
I need to feel that they are near me now;
I want them to know that I have begotten them, and that they,
too, are the fruit of my womb.
I want them to know that I am
more a woman than a virgin,
more a mother than a queen,
more theirs than yours,
because you did not create me for yourself but for them.
I want them to know that I am more revolutionary than
obedient because every true "Yes!" said to you
is a "No!" to all those acts of submission which enslave
men rather than free them.
You alone are the true liberator.
With you alone is man freer when he is obedient.
Therefore, I ask you today to correct the image that many
people have of me;
to destroy the physical and spiritual caricatures that they
have made of me;
to have them discover me as I am;
not to allow them to set me apart from their history or to
make me less human than themselves.
Do you know the keenest pain I feel now?
That those who say: "Christ, yes! The Church, no!" have no
place for me
in the building of a history made by men and for men.

At the very moment of liberation, why do they exclude me who gave flesh and blood to the only real Teacher of freedom?

The Farmer

Lord,
I am a farmer.
My face is brown and seamed like the earth.
For more than sixty years, I have seen the sun rise each
    morning,
    and I have watered the soil with the sweat of my brow.
But I have also felt the joy of savoring real things, and I seem to
    have found in them all the freshness of creation.
Am I mistaken, Lord, when I sense your presence in everything
    that my land gives me, that land of mine that has not yet
    been contaminated by the disgraceful exploitation of
    consumerism?
I have sensed your presence in the clear water of my wells and
    streams;
    in the bread which my wife baked in our kitchen, bread
    that was pure bread and nothing else;
    in the wine made from the grapes of my ripe, fruitful vine
    which is like a biblical poem.
I have sensed your presence when tasting the fruit of my cherry
    trees, my apple trees and my pear trees, and the products of
    my vegetable garden, which never lost the taste of the sun
    and the rain.
After sixty years of being close to the soil and its gifts, I now find

myself in the city,
where no one remembers the land, where no one is
interested in real bread and real wine.
My children thought that I would be better off here in the city,
where everything would be bigger, more amusing and more
convenient.
It's true that here they have more iron, more cement, more
people, more cars, more movie theaters,
more noise and more money . . . .
and also more churches.
But I can't pray, Lord.

I feel like rebelling against it all.
I can't sleep because I can hear the anguished lament of my
land, protesting and weeping as it is dragged through the
streets and marketplaces, humiliated and trying to hide its
shame, because society, in its pursuit of money, has
dishonored the best things in your creation.
Man should have continued the work that you began, by tilling
and enriching the soil, but he has instead misused and
misappropriated it.
Here the water is not the water that St. Francis of Assisi praised
so highly; instead, it is dirty and contaminated.
Here bread is no longer bread but a chemical product.
Here wine is no longer made with the grapes of our vines but is
just colored water.
Here fruit does not taste of the sun but seems to be made of
plastic and cotton wool.
Here everything tastes as if it had been concocted in a laboratory
and no longer savors of the earth.
Everything is tainted with lucre, speculation and exploitation.
So, Lord, let me shout out my sorrow.
Lend me for a moment the rage of your prophets, because I feel
like cursing.
I wouldn't curse technology and science if they served Nature by

perfecting it,
if they could multiply bread without making it cease being
bread, as you multiplied the loaves;
if they were able to work the miracle of bringing the fruits
of the earth to every table, but without having apples that
are no longer apples and without having potatoes lose the
taste of the good earth and milk the richness of lush grass.
In the manner of the ancient prophets, I curse the earth that has
been put at the service of lucre and not of life.
Since no one listens to me, and since everybody thinks I'm
crazy, let me cry out, at least to you, my indignation and
anguish. Lord, they are poisoning us!
Lord, I'm afraid that people will end up eating cement or
banknotes!
Lord, take up your whip again and go through the temple of
society, scourging the new money-changers. Cast them out,
because they are making your Father's house, this wide
world, a den of thieves, where it is no longer possible to
pray to Him who gives us our daily bread.

Pardon me, Lord, but I'm going away today; I'm leaving the city
and turning my back on "progress."
I'm shaking the dust from my feet, and I'm going back, a poor
man, to my land.
This is not cowardice or escapism or foolish nostalgia or a
condemnation of real progress.
Rather it is fear of losing my humanity;
it is fear of smelling too much of cement and hypocrisy;
it is fear of not being able to go on praying in the pure,
spare language of the earth, the sun, the wind and the rain;
it is fear of forgetting that man is worth more than what he
builds.
How could we go on being men if, subtly but diabolically, we
daily prostituted the earth which sustains our life and gives
us a deeper joy in the Incarnation?

Lord, when I'm on my land, although I may be poor and alone,
    I won't forget my neighbor.
Every morning at sunrise, I shall say this one prayer:
"May men still be able to savor the real taste of bread."

The Desperate

Lord,
we are the poor.
We come to you, the only one who will have anything to do with
    us,
    because you, too, were poor as we are, and because you love
    us.
It's not possible to love the poor without feeling, in some way,
    one with them.
We make up the great world of the unhappy,
    the desperate,
    the illiterate,
    the incurables,
    the lonely,
    the war-torn,
    the betrayed,
    the abnormal,
    those who have neither peace nor freedom,
    and those who have no faith.
All of us are burdened with the weight of a poverty that is not
    merely lack of money and that is frequently much worse
    because its roots go deeper.
Even without money a man can still love and believe, but
    without hope, all the money in the world is superfluous.

People who have no money are not the ones who most frequently commit suicide.

Instead, it is the incurably lonely, the desperate ones of the earth.

Therefore, we who have no hope feel that we are indeed the poorest of men.

I am a woman of fifty.

After thirty years of happy married life, my husband has gone to live with a young woman of twenty-five without even saying good-bye to me.

My life is finished, and I am merely going through the motions of living.

Who is poorer than I, Lord?

I am a young man.

I was blinded and lost both arms and most of both legs in an accident.

For the rest of my life, such as it is, I shall have to depend on other people for everything.

The hungriest street-urchin is richer than I.

Who would change his poverty for mine?

I am mentally ill.

I live in a psychiatric ward with others like me.

My few lucid moments are not a relief but an even greater cruelty because they allow me to see the plight I'm in.

I can scarcely call myself human any more.

I don't believe that there exists a poverty worse than mine.

I am a "lifer," a convict sentenced to life imprisonment without hope of parole.

I have no hope of ever walking down a street again as a free man because I committed a horrible crime: I murdered my wife and three children.

It was an act of madness done in a fury of jealousy; but the
    psychiatrists said I was legally sane when I did it.
My parents are both dead, and I have no brothers or sisters.
There is no one to pity me as I drag out my life here.
And no one will shed a tear for me when I die.
Who is poorer and more alone than I?

I am an ordinary worker.
The doctor has told me that I have inoperable cancer.
At most, I have a year to live, and then I'll die in atrocious pain.
When my wife heard about my illness, she started going around
    with other men, and she doesn't care what happens to me.
I have no children, and no faith.
Who would choose my kind of poverty?

I am a young girl, an orphan, not very pretty and, I've been told,
    not very bright.
An older man deceived me with promises of marriage, got me
    pregnant and then abandoned me in a strange city.
For a long time, I wasn't able to get work, and so I had to go on
    the streets.
The only thing that kept me going was my expected baby.
But now he has been born, and he's so deformed that even I can
    scarcely bear to look at him.
If I do succeed in finding the strength to carry on and not
    commit suicide, tell me, Lord, is there anyone poorer than
    I?
I feel as deformed as my child.

I am a Vietnamese girl.
I am twenty years of age.
As long as I can remember, I have heard the sound of guns and
    smelled the cordite.
I never knew my mother or my father.
All my life I seem to have seen nothing but uniforms.

I don't know what it is to be a woman, nor what love and peace are.

My heart is filled with hate, and my hands have held only dead bodies.

I curse the women who bear sons, for these sons will only grow up to be soldiers, to kill and be killed.

How much richer than I are even the inmates of an asylum!

I feel that I am the symbol of the vilest and most unjust poverty.

I don't even have a name.

For I was begotten of war and am owned by it.

And war will be my tomb.

Lord, I am poorer still.

I'm someone whom nobody has ever loved.

Does anyone know how lonely it is never to have received the smallest gesture of real love?

Never to have seen anyone looking at him tenderly?

How lonely it is never to have felt a hand stroking his brow with sympathy and kindness?

Or heard a friendly voice calling his name?

How lonely it is to know that he means nothing to anyone?

Believe me, Lord, that there is no loneliness, or sorrow, or poverty greater than ours, who have never been loved.

And we are legion.

All other kinds of poverty are basically wealth in comparison with ours if they include real love.

I would change places right now with the young man who had been blinded and maimed if I had someone near me to give my shattered body tender care and to say to me: "You are not alone. I love you!" I would willingly be the young Vietnamese girl if, even in the middle of war, I met a soldier who looked at me with true love or who, between bombing attacks, plucked a flower for me.

Of course, deep wounds are not suddenly and completely healed by the mere sound of a loving and consoling voice.

But it is even truer to say that all the riches and health and
peace in the world are the blackest and most oppressive
poverty if we have no one to say to us sincerely: "You are
not alone. I love you and need you!"

Well, Lord, I think that I am even poorer than those who have
never been loved.

I carry on my shoulders such a weight of misery, injustice,
betrayal and disillusionment that now the only words that
have any meaning for me are desperation, bitterness,
incredulity, mistrust, hatred, sorrow, pain, death and
suicide.

I would gladly change with anyone who still believes that a
gesture of love can have any value and who can hope to
receive one, even though his hope is really only wishful
thinking.

As for me, Lord, I don't believe in love anymore because I have
suffered so much and been betrayed so often that I have
lost the last shreds of faith.

I believe only in self-interest, which I know very well and which
has a thousand different faces, names and types.

Complete and utter desperation is my constant companion and
my daily bread.

And I don't know how long I can go on living with it.

Lord, I dare you to find someone poorer than I.

You came to free the poor especially; so can you, at least,
understand us?

But how can we believe that you love us when so many of us
curse you continually?

Reveal yourself once again and come to walk through our
streets, so that, from the depths of our wretchedness, we,
too, can cry out to you: "Have mercy on us, because we are
desperate!"

And don't delay, because we are losing the strength and even the
wish to call out to you.

Those Who Are Alone

We were eating in a small restaurant in the city.
There were six of us, strangers to each other, eating alone at
separate tables.
Nobody was smiling.
One was reading a newspaper while he ate, looking over the
theater and movie ads.
Another was on the phone for a long time, speaking very low.
But he didn't smile even once.
From time to time, glances met across the room, but the eyes
were not friendly.
As we sat eating, we were quite close to each other physically,
but in reality we were worlds apart.
Why, Lord?
Each of us ate quickly and then walked out, leaving a grudging
"Good night!" hanging in the air behind us.
Each of us seemed anxious to get away from the others into the
darkness of the city streets and to go in search of
his own answer,
his own hope,
his own work
or his own sin.
Why, Lord, were we so close and so distant at the same time?
Why is it so difficult for men to meet and be sociable even when

they have nothing against each other?

If someone had thrown a brick through the plate glass window of the restaurant, we would all have suddenly been drawn together and would have spoken to each other like friends.

Why is it that pain or shock unites people much faster than hope?

If one of us six had suddenly got ill then,
     our lives certainly would have been drawn together.

Most likely some of us would have gone to his aid, or called a doctor or even accompanied him home or to the hospital; and so we would have begun to get to know him and each other better.

But none of us needed the others: we simply ate our meal, paid for it and left.

None of us knew who his neighbor was.

Yet, Lord, was it true that we didn't need each other?

It is more than likely that all of us were Christians.

Perhaps all of us had gone to Mass the previous Sunday.

At least, we were all human beings, sons of the same soil, capable of giving and receiving and communicating with each other.

Perhaps each one of us was in need of a friendly word.

Perhaps one of us had the answer to another's problem.

Perhaps someone among us had the key to open the door of hope to the one who had been searching among the movie ads for a brief escape from his anxiety or disappointment.

Why is it so hard to believe that no one can walk beside us even for a short time without bringing us some of your riches?

Why is it so hard for us to believe that you can give us at every moment the word that our neighbor is hoping for and needs?

Is it not a fact that everyone is a gift for everyone else?

And yet we go on living together, eating together, taking the

same bus or elevator every day, without so much as greeting
each other,
exactly as if you had never walked the earth,
as if you had never risen from the dead,
as if you had not revealed to us that each man is you and
that there is a different "you" in each person,
as if we had forgotten that what one man can give us,
another has not yet offered,
as if we did not believe that we shall become mature only to
the degree in which we open ourselves to each and every
one,
as if the responsibility for taking the first step did not rest
on each of us.
Why, Lord, is it easy to make friends on the battlefield or in a
hospital ward, while it is so difficult to do so when there is
peace in our streets, when we can enjoy the sun and eat a
leisurely meal or have a quiet drink together?
Is it possible, Lord, for us to be Christians and still be unable to
meet each other, to shake hands,
to begin a human dialogue, to wish each other a sincere
"Good night!"
as should be the case with men who are eternally bound
together in one and the same destiny?

Lord, at least let us not forget that we are men.
Let us not wait to remember that we are brothers until war
breaks out or tragedy strikes.
Let us not regard friendship as being only a winter fruit.

The Pope

Lord,
many people think that it must be very easy for a pope to pray,
because they don't realize that a pope is a man, weak and alone,
　　like everyone else;
　　　　because they think that I have an open line to you and that
　　　　I'm like a secretary to whom you dictate your wishes.
They're convinced that I'm never in doubt and never afraid that
　　I may be mistaken.
Lord, I wish I could say my prayers aloud in the marketplaces of
　　the world so that people could see that, when I pray, I, too,
　　feel the anger of the ancient prophets, your sorrow over
　　Jerusalem, the torture of your abandonment on the Cross,
　　and not the rapture of Mount Tabor.
I know, Lord, that many people doubt that my prayer can be
　　like that of the saints of the Old Testament,
　　　　because they think that I do not feel the joy and the
　　　　challenge of Abraham's great venture,
　　　　while, on the other hand, others doubt that my prayer can
　　　　be an echo of the prayer said by Peter, who felt so keenly
　　　　the responsibility and inerrancy of his decisions.
But I can't pray in public as I do in private, Lord, because
　　history has made Peter's successor
　　　　into a remote, god-like figure who cannot confess either his

joys or his anxieties.

I am aware that there are many who would rather die than see
the pope in any other light,
many who regard him more as a "presence" than as a
person.

Many don't know that being pope today is like selling oneself
into slavery
and resigning oneself to a life of perpetual contradiction,
continual paradox
and almost impossible balance.

I wonder, Lord, if that is to be my cross?

I feel that it is my lot to be stretched on the rack of ceaseless
questions that torture me day and night.

Must it be like that, Lord? Or is my distress sheerly the result of
my own weakness?

That is the most tormenting question of all.

I'd like to begin my prayer today with your words in the Garden
of Gethsemane:

"If it be possible, let this chalice pass from me," especially if this
is not a chalice that you have prepared for me, but one that
I have filled for myself.

If this cross is not yours but one of my own making, take it away
from me, because, in spite of what my detractors say, the
whole trend of my personality is towards joy and
resurrection.

I know that spiritual pessimism is not Christian, and that it
should have no place in the life of a pope.

But I want my prayer, like yours, to be complete.

Rather than betray my mission,
or turn a deaf ear to your call,
or mar even slightly the beauty of your spouse, the Church,
I repeat: "Thy will be done!"

I shall accept not only the pain of contradiction and anxiety, but
also the humiliation of appearing before the world with the

worry of unsolved problems written clearly on my face.

Wouldn't this be the sincerest and humblest confession I could make of my essential poverty?

Lord, I know that my place is in the center of the community that you have confided to me.

In a very real way, I am like the hearth around which the family gathers to warm themselves, to rest, to regain their strength and to plan for the future.

Lord, why do I often feel so terribly alone?

Is it my own fault, or are others to blame?

Must a pope feel alone?

Do I feel alone because it is people who have drawn away from me, or because it is I who don't know how to get close to them?

Lord, do you, at least, understand my pain?

I am convinced that my vocation and mission is to be the visible and tangible symbol of the essential unity of your Church, of unity in plurality.

Even before you called me to be the successor of St. Peter, you had already made me feel that I had been called to try to reconcile the apparently irreconcilable.

But, Lord, although I have a burning desire for unity, why do you allow the diabolical word "schism" to echo around the world, in my pontificate and on my very own lips?

Lord, I cannot rest while there is a possibility of a new break in unity,

when you yourself prayed so fervently that all of us might be one.

Don't you see, Lord, that if a new schism appears in the Church, I shall have to be the first to plead guilty before the tribunal of your justice?

Because guilt in these matters is never one-sided, and because, in conscience, I shall have to assume the greater part of the responsibility.

Since the world today is skeptical about mere words, I have tried
to speak with the more expressive and more effective
language of action:
I left aside the tiara to show my willingness to serve instead of
ruling;
I became a pilgrim to tell the world that I wanted to meet
everyone, without distinction of race or religion;
I left my home to visit those who had become separated from us,
to show my desire for reconciliation without making
demands that are humiliating and against the spirit of the
Gospel;
I offered my home as a place where the peoples of Vietnam
could negotiate the peace that the world needs,
so that it would be clear that the Church was more
interested in peace than in the prestige of her diplomatic
structures.
I went against the wishes of many of my advisers by reforming
the Curia, setting up the synod of bishops and creating the
secretariates for dialogue with those who do not think as we
do, in order to show my willingness to open a new page in
the government of the Church.
And many people did see my actions as a hopeful beginning:
above all, the humble and the poor, who look hopefully to
the liberating power of the Church.

My actions were effective, it is true, but what about my words?
I cannot speak with actions alone; I must proclaim, defend and
stimulate the Faith.
But, while my actions promoted freedom and gave rise to hope,
I was distressed to find that, very often, my words aroused
bitterness, anger and disappointment in all ranks of society.
My actions angered mostly the influential people; but my words
disturbed the weak as well and were often used by those
who wished to stop the process of liberation.
Should I be silent, Lord?

Should I speak less, Lord?

Are the times such that I should go on speaking with actions
  instead of words?

Would the Dutch people have understood better my desire not
  to break off the dialogue if I had taken the first plane to
  Utrecht
  instead of dictating a letter to my secretary?

I know, Lord, that for many people my words no longer have
  any value because they deny that I have the charism of
  strengthening in the Faith, that charism which you wished
  to give me as Peter's successor.

Yet others regard my words too highly and confuse them with
  yours.

Perhaps I am paying the price for the sin which history
  committed by identifying Peter's successor with you, as if
  you had handed in your resignation,
  as if you yourself did not continue to rule the Church,
  as if the only definitive word was not always yours, which
  mine were only meant to serve?

Help me, Lord, so that my words may be as liberating as my
  actions.

And if that is not possible, I'd prefer to remain silent.

I tremble at the thought that even one man should be enchained
  and cheated by my words,
  that even one true prophet should have his charism
  slighted, that even one struggling man should lose hope.

For if my words are not capable of creating freedom, what
  assurance do I myself have of being an heir to that freedom
  which you revealed and gave to us?

The world is afraid, Lord.

Even the great are fearful.

The little ones of the earth accept fear as their daily bread, and
  consequently they are always expecting the arrival of a new
  messiah.

I cannot forget the look on those millions of faces which crowded around me as I traveled through the world.

They were crying out to me with their eyes that they were afraid, that they were searching for hope.

Many of them were poor because they lacked bread, while others were poor because they lacked God.

I know that I am not you, but they confused me with you in their desperate efforts to find you as the foundation of their hope.

I must assure them that their hope is not an empty one;

I must make them feel that fear is irrational because you exist and have conquered death.

The more fear menaces the world, the more I must cry out that our confidence has a name, your name, and that no one, therefore, can kill it.

We who believe in you cannot permit ourselves the luxury of fear,

because we must show in our lives that love casts out fear and that we are not believing and trusting in something that is impossible.

But I must confess, Lord, that sometimes I myself am afraid.

I am not ashamed of my weakness; I am not humiliated at finding that I am just one more in the long line of those who feel the icy hand of fear gripping their hearts.

Yet I cannot allow the weak ones of the earth to see my fear because that would increase theirs;

and I know that if I do not proclaim hope at all costs, many will turn their backs on you as their last hope of freeing themselves from panic.

A pope can permit himself only one fear:

that of not being able to reveal to humanity that our faith in love works the impossible miracle of freeing men from the fear that paralyzes them and makes it impossible for them to fulfill themselves completely;

the fear that he might be tempted to try to banish men's

fear by an ill-considered act of authority.

Lord, why do you allow pessimism to weigh me down sometimes
as I sit at my desk,
while millions of men beseech me, at least, to go on
proclaiming that fear is not Christian?

You know that I am poor,
poorer than many workers and many farmers,
for I don't even have a life of my own.
I can never be myself,
but must always be the Pope.

Lord, very few people understand the poverty and deprivation of
having one's every word and action observed, analyzed and
used by someone for his own purposes.

I have the impression that every television camera in the world
is focused on my every move.

When I speak, I feel that I am talking into all the microphones
of the world.

I am poorer, much poorer, than my chauffeur.

But can the poor of the world see and appreciate my poverty?
It's hard to live in a prison, but it's even harder to live there
when everyone is convinced that one is living in a palace.

What shall I do, Lord?

If I break with old customs and go to live as a simple parish
priest somewhere in Rome, many people will rend their
garments and say that the pope has gone mad.

And if I accept the contradiction of my golden poverty, perhaps
the poor of the world will never be able to recognize me as
the successor of St. Peter, who miraculously cured them in
your name precisely because he had neither gold nor silver.

Do you see my dilemma, Lord?

Do you think that, when I was signing my encyclical on the
development of the poor nations of the world, I did not feel
the bitter contrast between what I had just written and the
society in which I had written it,

a society which lives and feeds on the very wellsprings of injustice that I had condemned as meriting your anger?

Lord, how can I be both the pope of dialogue and the pope of radical decisions made against the wishes of my closest collaborators, who do not think as I do?

How can I be both the pilgrim of Nazareth, stripped of all the weight of temporal power, and the chief of state, although this state is more symbolical than real?

How can I harmonize gospel simplicity with the murky world of mundane diplomacy in which the pope must frequently move?

If the Gospel is radical, with its clear-cut "Yes" and "No" answers, how can the pope be both diplomatic and true to the Gospel?

For, as you know very well, Lord, in diplomacy, "Yes" can also mean "No," and "No" can be very like "Yes."

And the weak distrust diplomacy as a game played by the powerful,
while they welcome sincerity as a sign of hope.

They do not fear the truth, for they know by instinct that the Truth became poor and belongs to them.

Why cannot I truly be the pope of the oppressed?

Few understand my suffering at having to be Peter while I feel the call to be Paul.

Deep within me, Lord, I feel the need and the vocation to open up a road for you through the Babel of the modern world, as Paul did through the confusion of the pagan world.

But opening new roads can give the impression of breaking with the past and can arouse a fear which opportunists may turn to their own advantage, while they accuse me of betraying Peter.

It is not easy to be at once a rock and a boat, a prophet and a superior.

My hesitation and my dilemmas are the result of my desire to reconcile the two duties that preoccupy me, namely, to defend the Faith and to break new ground.

It's true that, in Jerusalem, Peter gave in to Paul.

But how can I back down before myself?

Must I make a choice?

As you know, Lord, and as I painfully acknowledge, my problem is that what I say is not acceptable either to those who take St. Paul as their model or to those who follow St. Peter in the two dimensions, faithfulness to dogma and the need to take account of the new problems of today.

Actually, Lord, I don't know what to pray to you for.

Today everybody is preaching the need to free man's conscience, the urgency to recover the biblical concept of conscience as synonymous with the authentic voice of God in the depths of our hearts, where he Has written His fundamental law of love.

What about the Pope's conscience?

Can I renounce my own conscience to follow that of the majority of the community?

But how am I to distinguish, Lord, between my personal conscience as a Christian

and my obligation to respect and enlighten the consciences of other men?

Faced as I am with this conflict, this doubt, this need to supply an answer or make a decision for the whole community, what must I do, Lord?

I am well aware of the temptation to impose my personal solution to a problem on the whole community,

even in those things which are not defined by the Faith or sufficiently well developed.

What do you think, Lord?

Is it better for me to wait before coming to a decision so that I can have time to measure my personal conscience against the conscience of the community, or can I trust my personal conscience and impose it on others in order to prevent problems from piling up without solutions?

In any case, Lord, don't let me forget that, although my word must always be the last word, it need not inevitably be the second-to-the-last word also, nor must it necessarily be quite different from what everyone else is saying.

Yet, Lord, how can a pope, living in his golden prison, really know how certain problems are viewed by the great mass of those who do not speak,

of those who make up the best and healthiest part of your Church because they are the last of all,

those who will never get near me,

those who are so easily used,

those who can't defend themselves when they are made to say what they never believed?

How can I ignore the fact that news is almost always "filtered" before it reaches the pope?

When I want to know what a certain part of your Church thinks, how can I do so without having recourse to the information supplied by those very sources which treat your Church with scant love and respect?

You are aware how difficult it is to know the whole truth about anything even when the source is trustworthy, because, with the best will in the world, every one of us "filters" and interprets it.

What, then, can a poor pope do since the news that reaches him, when it does reach him, is slanted or colored, interpreted or explained away?

Gloomy reports of the ills of the Church seem to have no difficulty in reaching the pope,

while only too seldom does he hear about the faithfulness of so many ordinary people,

their hidden goodness, their silent hopes, their sincere predictions, their sympathetic voices saying to him:

"Don't be afraid! Don't be sad! Don't be discouraged!

Christ has not died. No one can bury His name or His truth because, if necessary, the very stones would proclaim Him."

Lord, may I never betray the tired but prophetic voice of that great world of the silent.

Give me the chance to hear that voice.

Give me the courage to prefer that voice because, more than any other, it is yours.

Give me faith in the truth of that voice.

Condemn me to silence rather than allow me to betray its words of life.

If I must scandalize someone when I am making my difficult choices of conscience, let me scandalize the great, the tyrants, the exploiters, the inquisitors.

I cannot forget, Lord, that Peter, too, fell into the temptation to keep the little ones away from Christ to leave more room for the great.

And remind me at every moment that your kingdom continues to be, above all, the kingdom of those who never speak.

Those Who Say Nothing

Lord,
we are the silent ones of the world,
those who have never had the right or the courage to speak,
those who have always had to put up with listening to
others.
Lord, is this because what we have to say is useless and of no
account?
I feel that life is passing me by in a mad rush. There is no place
for me in the councils of those who speak and make all the
decisions.
I see many injustices done to me and to others, but I am unable
to do anything about it.
Those who are in power are well aware of my weakness, and
instead of holding out a helping hand to me, they use me
for their own purposes by putting words into my mouth or
making decisions that I have never even thought of, much
less shared in.
I confess, Lord, that I'm afraid to speak and that I don't know
how to stop others from making use of my silence.
When shall we silent people find the strength to express aloud
all the cares and worries that we have been carrying in our
hearts for centuries?
Lord, my prayer is nothing but a cry for help to discover my

human dignity, which has been ignored or pushed aside by all the influential people and all the institutions, including even the one which should have handed on to me your message of liberation.

Lord, do you really want to know why I'm so afraid, why I have no confidence in myself, why I think that what others say or do is always better than anything I could say or do?

Do you want to know why I have given up trying and resigned myself to my fate?

And why I am convinced that all I can hope for are a few crumbs of life, like poor Lazarus at the rich man's door?

The answer is very simple, Lord:

I am as I am because I was born among the poor and the powerless, and because I learned from the cradle that I simply don't count, and that only those who own things can make themselves respected and have a right to happiness.

At home, they always told me that I had to be contented with my lot and that I could only look forward to what they had had—slavery.

Time and time again, my mother and father told me that I must keep my mouth shut and say nothing whenever someone rich and powerful was speaking, because I couldn't possibly know anything.

And although my mother loved me dearly, it was she who did most damage to me in this respect,

no doubt because she was so anxious to keep me out of trouble.

Then I went to school.

There the only time the teacher deigned to speak to me from his intellectual heights was when he wanted to tell me how ignorant, stupid and hopeless I was.

Almost the only thing I learned from him was that history had been made by a handful of great men and that the rest of us had done nothing and could expect nothing.

Then I went to catechism class.

And there, Lord, I discovered that not only was I a thick-headed
fool without any rights, but that I was also a sinner.

Everything I was inclined to say, do or think was evil and
deserving of hell,

so that the only safe course for me was to say nothing and
do nothing, not even think.

And if my body or mind cried out for something, I had to
mortify myself since I could aspire to nothing, because I
was stained with sin.

Your priests did all they could to drum into me the lesson that
man could do nothing without you and that you freely
choose those you wish to help, and that the saints were
great because you had selected them for greatness.

As for me, Lord, I had little enough to look forward to, even in
the next life.

As I grew from infancy to childhood to youth, my self-esteem
was gradually being whittled away.

Yet I still had one faint hope,

the hope that when I grew up, people would respect me.

I thought that perhaps one day I too would be able to say
something important . . .

But the factory was waiting to finish me off.

There the bosses bought most of my time and my freedom for a
crust of bread.

I tried to rebel, but my fellow-slaves asked me what I was trying
to do, and when I replied timidly that I wanted to preserve
my self-respect, they laughed in my face and reminded me
that the teacher had always said that I was a fool.

They told me that no one could defend his rights single-
handedly and that that was what the union was for.

The union officials knew what to do, and who was I to think
and act for myself?

At the age of twenty, I went into the army and learned to say:

"Yes, sir!",

which didn't cost me a thought . . . .

because I was already well used to doing what other people wanted.

When I was twenty-one, I was handed a ballot paper and told to vote, because every citizen is free to partake in the democratic election of his political representatives.

When I went into the polling booth, I was thinking about you, Lord, when I marked my "X" on the ballot paper. You were nailed to a cross for having dared to say that every man is free, that every man is God. and then I was able to pluck up the courage to speak to you, at least.

But I know that this is not enough.

I must have the courage to speak to every man.

I must have the courage to fight side by side with all those who believe, not only in you, but also in me. We must fight so that all the world may hear the voice of those who are silent because they are afraid to speak or are forced to keep quiet.

Although I have been silent so long, I have little to say now, and the little I do have to say is the only prayer I can address to you, the Word who was made flesh to free men:

"We've had enough of fear, enough of resignation, enough of the injustice that has turned so many people into dull, uncomplaining cattle like me!"

The Rebel

Lord,
I am not happy with the way things are.
They call me a revolutionary.
I'm convinced that life on earth could be better than it is.
I have to rise up against every kind of injustice, beginning with
the injustice that I feel within me.
I know that it would be easier and less of an effort to let things
stay as they are, but if I did that I would never have any
happiness or peace.
Lord, they tell me that everything that exists is sacred; but I feel
that this statement may merely be a justification for all
forms of laziness and compromise.
I believe that we all have the sacred right to improve on or
perfect what we already possess. .
My vocation is to struggle against oppression of every kind and
to promote everything that is liberating.
I know very well, Lord, that, for many people, a revolutionary is
also a destroyer.
But I believe that it is not possible to be creative without being a
revolutionary.
They tell me that one must first build before destroying.
But isn't it good to destroy things that bring death, ruin and
oppression?

It is always good to destroy a cancer, because that means giving
  a man new life.
My revolution, Lord, is worldwide because the degradation of
  man by structures is worldwide, too.
And total revolution is hard on everyone, myself most of all,
  because we all feel inclined to defend our false feeling of
  tranquillity and save ourselves all the toil and fatigue that is
  inseparable from any creative act.
Lord, they say that I am violent.
But my violence is not turned against man but against every
  system of oppression that victimizes man.
Yet what am I to do
  when the oppressive powers and structures are represented
  and defended by men who say that they are legitimate and
  necessary?
Lord, Herod was a man, and you called him a fox; Peter was a
  man and one of your own apostles, and you called him a
  devil; the priests and the Pharisees were men of flesh and
  blood, and you called them vipers; the money-changers in
  the Temple were men, and you threw them out violently.
Am I to resign myself to things as they are?
Am I to wait for justice to fall into our laps?
Am I to stand idly by and see millions of men suffer and grow
  desperate because of a few tyrants?
Isn't it lawful to fight against those who have arrogated to
  themselves the right to decide for everyone else, to exploit
  and oppress them?
These tyrants have forgotten even their own humanity, and this
  is why the long procession of the poor and enslaved of the
  world no longer regard them as men but as the incarnation
  of evil.
How can I save these tyrants, too?
How am I to defend myself from them without betraying all the
  oppressed?
What can I save from a society that grants only to a few the

right to a real life?

How is it possible today to love men without feeling impelled to bring about a total transformation of society?

How is it possible not to be violent in this world of violence?

It is true that it's not easy to select the means of revolution that will ensure the justice and effectiveness of my revolt.

And it is equally true that brainless violence could cause a wave of even harsher slavery.

But these difficulties and problems of conscience must not be an excuse for passivity and compromise.

That would be an even greater betrayal.

Lord, although I am not always sure of the means I must use to bring about reform, I know that my decision to change things is the only possible one for me as a man since the freedom and dignity of all other men are identical with mine.

Lord, you haven't given us any sure, definite means of bringing about a revolution at every moment of history.

But the call to fight against injustice of every kind is clear in your words and your life.

You yourself always used the means that you thought most suitable and effective, but you did not impose them as the only possible ones.

We have to create and invent our own means, with honesty and sincerity.

I know that a mistake here could be grave and most painful.

But aren't fear and the lack of faith and courage even more so?

Lord, my fear is not so great as to stop me from seeing clearly which are the most effective means for carrying out my project.

My real fear is the subtle, diabolical temptation to use the revolution for my own advantage instead of putting it at the service of the rest of men.

I don't want to start a revolution to grab power for myself, but to

use that power in the service and for the betterment of all.
I don't want to start a revolution so that I can live out the rest of
my life in secure happiness.
If a revolution is to be real, it must be a continuous fight and
effort, because men are continually tempted to seize the
rights of others, to poison the wellspring of creative love and
to frustrate any attempts at true humanity.
For me, Lord, revolution means to be always on the watch so
that the wolves cannot enter the sheepfold, and it is not
even enough to do that, since many of the sheep are
tempted to become wolves themselves.

Revolution can and must be continuous because it was you,
Lord, who revealed to us man's infinite creative
possibilities.
And this faith in man is the motivating force behind my
revolution.
Do you agree, Lord?
I'd like to know what you meant when you said:
"I have not come to bring peace but the sword."
"I have come to set father against son."
"The kingdom of heaven suffers violence, and the violent bear it
away."
"He who loves his life shall lose it."
"Woe to you rich!"
I'd like to know *your* interpretation of those words and not that
of the commentators, who, since they found that they could
not ignore these words of yours, at least tried to water them
down and use them for the benefit of the self-satisfied, the
lazy and the well-entrenched.

The Soldier

Lord,
I am a young soldier.

Since I've been in the army, I've found it harder to pray than
    before, perhaps because they sometimes make me go to
    church, or because I'm being destroyed as a person.

Lord, I don't know if it's because I'm angry or because I'm sad,
    but I feel the need to pray to you today.

Perhaps you will understand me because you experienced in your
    own flesh how a soldier can be brutalized to such an extent
    that he no longer respects the dignity of another man.

On the night before your death, a crowd of soldiers struck you
    in the face and made a mockery of your dignity as a man,
    treating you like a puppet on a string.

Lord, a short while ago I was scandalized when I heard that
    some young men like me had chosen to go to prison rather
    than serve an apprenticeship to war by doing their military
    service.

But now I'm beginning to be scandalized at myself and at all the
    others like me who passively accept this state of affairs.

Hence, Lord, I want to begin my prayer to you, the Author of
    life and the Prince of peace, by begging you to give me and
    others like me the strength to react against being compelled
    to learn how to kill.

Why is our fear to resist even stronger than our love for life?

Do you think that the young men of today would go to war if they were left to themselves and not pushed into it?

No, we're not like that.

It is others who have reduced us to such a state of insensitivity.

Lord, give us the strength to regain our original enthusiasm for everything that favors life and not death.

Help us to understand the extent to which we have been brainwashed by false logic to prepare us for war.

They have made the idea of patriotism sacred so that we'll forget that the only philosophy which counts is that which respects the life of each and every man.

They call us to arms and preach about defending the sacred soil of the homeland;

and even our own parents ask us what we would do if they were attacked by the enemy.

They try to make us see that you haven't lived unless you've been a soldier, and they tell us: "Anyone who hasn't been in the army doesn't know what life is really like!"

Our own family assures us, sometimes a little maliciously, that: "They'll teach you discipline in the army. They'll teach you how to say: 'Yes, sir!' "

We're given to understand that a spell in the army is necessary if we are to become mature; and we're told that it is our sacred duty to wage war in defense of our national institutions.

That is what our elders tell us.

But now, Lord, listen to what I, a poor recruit, have to say about my first experience of the army.

Let me tell you while I can, before it is too late and before I become hardened like so many others and unable to react normally.

The minute you enter, Lord, they shove you into a uniform to let you know that you are no longer you but only an object, a thing;

and that you have lost your most elementary rights.

For a couple of years, you have to forget that you are a human being, a person, capable of loving, thinking, feeling, and being respected.

They can do things to you with impunity that they could never do if you weren't a soldier.

They tell you not to think, because that's a sin for a soldier.

And there's a whole series of rules and punishments which they're ready to spring on you to see if you are a thing yet or if you still retain some vestiges of humanity.

Under those conditions, Lord, how can I pray to you?

How can I pray when they are destroying me so thoroughly that I don't even know who I am any longer.

And when they have destroyed me spiritually, intellectually and even physically—since pain doesn't matter to a machine—then the monster that they have made of me is ready to learn how to kill and even to organize others to kill.

In these circumstances, where am I to find you, Lord?

Is there really any place for you in our barracks?

The very presence among us of our chaplain, your representative, is a scandal because in your Gospel of freedom and humanity there is no place for men who are important only to the extent that they are prepared to kill their fellowmen.

And what do the head of state and his generals look so pleased about when we parade fully armed before them?

Is it because they are glad to see that the man who was in us is now destroyed and that we have become so many machines, ready to kill at their orders?

Lord, it is useless for those who prepare and command us to kill to try to justify themselves by saying that we have a right to defend ourselves.

Nowadays people are becoming increasingly aware that there are other weapons against unjust aggression, namely, the spreading consciousness of man's dignity and of what is just and unjust.

A community's values cannot be defended by snapping to attention and saying: "Yes, sir!", or by demanding "a tooth for a tooth," but by the universal recognition of the dignity of every human community.

When a community is faced with unjust aggression, it should cry out to the whole world: "If I have done evil, tell me what it is. But if not, then why do you strike me?"

Of course, those who believe only in the force of arms will laugh at these words.

But I cannot forget that they are your words, which you used when you were condemned to death and when you refused to be defended by the swords of your friends.

Yet who decides that we have been the victims of unjust aggression?

All we soldiers have to do is to obey orders, although we know from history that most wars were not fought as a just defense but rather as economic, ideological or political strategy.

Lord, let me point out a few unpleasant truths to our parents, not to accuse them of doing anything wrong, since they, too, have been used and taken in, but only to make them wake up to reality. It's pointless for you, our parents, to go on bringing sons into the world only to see them taken from you, turned into machines, and then ordered to kill the sons of other parents.

You are the wellsprings of life and the custodians of love, so why don't you fight more fiercely against the scandal of a system that turns the fruit of your love into weapons of war?

If mothers are not capable of rebelling against war of all kinds and against any kind of apprenticeship to war, then mankind does not have much of a future.

You mothers of the world ought to be the most strenuous conscientious objectors rather than allow the sons of your wombs to leave home and enter the most absurd school imaginable, the school that teaches your sons to kill the sons of other mothers.

Christ, forgive me if my prayer is a harsh one and full of the violence of the strong life that hammers in my veins.

Yet my prayer is not a condemnation of anyone in particular, but rather a cry of anguish and of hope to remind those who are responsible for the present system—of whom I am the first because of my cowardly silence—that man was created for life and for living together, for dialogue and for love.

No, if you want peace, preparing for war is not the way to get it!

It would be diabolical to say that it is.

Instead, the contrary is true: real peace can be attained only if recourse to arms is completely rejected.

If we lay aside our arms, innocent blood will continue to flow, perhaps for a long time to come.

But it is only through innocence, freely immolated, that humanity will find the superhuman strength needed to show the utter futility of all war.

Invoking self-defense as a justification for war is the clearest proof of our failure to hope and trust in the dignity of man and in his deepest conscience.

It is to go on believing that, in the end, the evil in man will always emerge triumphant.

But I believe, Lord, that the victory will go to the good that lies hidden in every man's heart, and that recourse to arms will never bring this goodness to light.

The Devil

Christ,
I am the devil, evil personified.
I live side by side with you in the hearts of men.
I am the weed that grows with the wheat.
I know that the final victory will be yours, but there are still
    many people who do not believe in that final victory, which
    is already a reality.
I feel that such people are already mine, in part at least.
I know that I am defeated every time a man consents to be a
    god, not as a conquest, but as a gift.
Yet my victory will last in those who go on wanting to be gods
    on their own account, and who are willing to bite into any
    magic apple to attain that goal.
My victory will be final in those who want to become gods in
    order to know evil, and in those who are afraid to accept
    the greatness of being gods.
The former are basically ashamed of being men, while the latter
    are afraid to be gods.
There are only two types of human beings who do not and will
    never fear me:
    the first are the tyrants, the self-satisfied and the loners, that
    is, those who are afraid of love; these do not fear me,
    because they *are* me!

the second are the oppressed, the poor, the liberated, that is, those who never lose the ability to hope, who believe in love; these do not fear me, because they are *you!*

I cannot pray to you because evil cannot kneel before good and because the good can be petitioned only for man's freedom, whereas I love chains and enslavement.

But the truth is that every man is half God and half Satan.

Therefore, men often pray to you for what is evil, as Peter did when he begged you not to be faithful to your mission and not to give your life for men.

And for that, you called him Satan.

Yes, when man prays to you through my lips and on behalf of the weeds that are growing among the wheat, he prays in this diabolical fashion:

May men never discover the joy of being men;
    may they lose the hope of being free;
    may they give up trying to create a world where neither power nor avarice nor ambition is necessary for happiness;
    may they continue to convince themselves that the equality of all men, brought about without hate and with only the violence of love, is an unattainable, utopian dream.

If they do this, then war is assured, and not just any kind of war but that most marvelous of all wars, civil war.

May they lose the hope of ever being able to build their own world together as brothers, without acting like sheep;
    may they value lone effort more than community endeavor, competition   more than solidarity.

In this way, I shall be assured of alienation, desperation, drug addiction, suicide and disunity, all of which are especially mine.

May they never lose their love and esteem for money, and may all of them, even your followers, remain convinced that everything, including you, can be bought.

May they never discover that conscience is surer and more

faithful than the law, so that the newness and force of your Gospel may be hidden, and so that the sins of the virtuous, which never break the law but which gnaw at their consciences, may go on multiplying.

For I know very well that the law does not save and that conscience frees, because you chose the spirit over the letter of the law.

May they go on being afraid of conquering the earth and of creating a new world, because only then shall I have greater scope for making them fear me, and in this way I shall be assured of skepticism, laziness and corruption.

May they go on fearing pornography more than injustice; may they continue to defend dogmas more than they stand up for the poor and the oppressed;

may they go on fighting more for their own individual freedom than for the freedom of all;

may they continue to love you while they forget about loving men.

In this way I shall be assured of your death in the world.

May they go on praising and canonizing the man whom you condemned in the parable of the talents; the one who was afraid of you and didn't dare risk losing his single talent; the one who personifies the prudence of the flesh, which kills every personal initiative; the one who always has to wait for directions before he can fulfill himself.

In this way, they'll end up by convincing themselves that they must leave your Church if they are to build their own world.

May they never discover that in the parable of the talents you didn't mention the man who stakes everything he has and loses it. If they realize that you did not condemn such a man, they will know that you have given them the maximum of freedom to risk all,

and that they won't need to leave your Church in order to

be themselves
and to walk out in front of the rest without fear of defeat.
May they go on believing that salvation is attainable only by
human efforts and human means.
In this way, I shall be assured that they will use their fellowmen
and will sell, betray and forget them in order to ensure your
benevolence for themselves.
May they go on adoring you as God, while forgetting that you
are also man,
so that they will not be capable of discovering that you are
still being put to death, not by those who don't believe in
God, but by those who don't believe in man.
In this way, the process of liberating everything human will be
stopped. In this way, they will never know you. In this way,
Christianity will go on being unintelligible to the majority
of men.
In this way, I shall be sure that men will end up by losing their
own identities and becoming neither gods nor men but
monsters.

I know that you won't listen to my prayer,
but can you deny that many of your followers will go on
praying to you like that and will force others to do so too?
To that extent at least, I have defeated you!

The Politician

Lord,
I am a politician,
that is to say, one of the least-loved people in present-day society.
Today nobody believes in us politicians, although they may fear
and fawn upon us.
And this is tragic because many of us chose to become
politicians out of a sincere desire to serve and get justice for
our people.
This is only the simple truth, as you know, Lord.
But I must confess with shame and sorrow that for most of us
politics has become a more or less studied disregard for the
very people we set out to serve.
When we entered politics, certain words such as "the people,"
"justice," and "freedom," were dear to us and were the very
heart of our program.
Unfortunately, too often there is only one word which means
anything to the hardened politician, and that word is
"power," which is precisely the thing that you came to
criticize and reject so that a new humanity could be born,
one in which men could meet each other and live together,
working side by side and serving each other, instead of
trying to dominate their fellowmen.
We are now paying a heavy price for disregarding the people,

because by doing so, we are betraying ourselves and making it impossible for us to be ourselves. We are living a lie.

We are so many little tin gods because, instead of devoting our lives to the service of our fellowmen, we are making them serve us.

And we don't realize that this is turning us into little slaves, without any lives of our own.

We grab power with both hands and hug it to us as the booty due us, and we imagine that we, of all men, are the freest.

In reality who is more enslaved than we, the professional politicians?

What greater slavery is there than to be openly branded as hypocrites by so many people?

Lord, I'm beginning to feel the weight of these chains which I have forged for myself and which are even heavier than those the people have to wear.

That is why I have decided to pray to you.

There's a question I want to ask you, Lord, and it is this: why do we politicians go on acting as we do, although we fully realize the terrible situation we're in?

Have we lost the ability to see things as they really are?

I don't want to justify myself or my fellow politicians, but I must at least ask myself what kind of system have we become embroiled in, since it seems to be stronger than even the best of men?

What is the temptation that lies in wait for the politician when he first enters the system, a temptation so powerful that he ends up by pitilessly forgetting those whom he set out to serve?

Lord, I think it is the sweet, subtle temptation to feel like God for once in his life.

It is the allurement of being able to decide the future of other men.

And it is the most dangerous of temptations because it has all the appearances and all the characteristics of "service" to others.

Hence it is difficult to censure the politician as such.

Power is very alluring, and, to avoid losing it, we are capable of betraying everything that we hold most sacred, including conscience, friendship and justice.

Our conscience will go on reminding us of our betrayal, but we shall try to lull it to sleep by persuading ourselves that, if we do our job well, we shall be rendering the best service to our fellowmen. But we forget that our job also requires continual, disinterested self-sacrifice, which is very difficult indeed.

Hence we are constantly tempted to commit the worst crime of all by making men serve us, arrogating to ourselves the very thing that makes men human, the power to decide for themselves. And as a result, we feel that we are "supermen."

Taking over other men's freedom is the most intoxicating, but also the most subtle and dangerous temptation.

And it is, above all, a terrible illusion, because when we have taken away our fellowmen's capacity to decide their own destiny, thereby making them mere objects to be manipulated, the freedom that we have taken to ourselves is of no use to us.

Even more, it shackles our own freedom.

This is the greatest punishment for our thirst for power, although it is very painful for us to admit it.

The public often regard us politicians as licensed thieves because they are aware that we rob them of their greatest treasure, their ability to plan their lives.

Lord, we are continually confusing politics with power, whereas in reality they are two completely different things, as different from each other as are power and authority.

Even the man in the street today accepts this confusion as

inevitable and generally regards a politician as a powerful man. The ordinary people are so convinced of this that they can see no other course but to surrender.

What are we to do when our consciences begin to show us the dirty game we're playing?

Is it still possible, in the world of today, to be a politician in the best sense of the word, that is to say, to live for the service of the people so as to guarantee and defend their inalienable right to plan their own lives in freedom, and to foster continually both personal and community creativity?

Is it possible to fight sincerely for the betterment of mankind by progressing from an anonymous collectivity, based on the power of a few, to a truly universal community, founded on a meeting of minds, fraternal collaboration and respect for personal liberty?

Many people still think that such things are possible.

And I respect their opinion.

But personally, as a result of my long, tragic experience, I am very much afraid that this hope is only an evasion or an attempt at self-justification in order not to lose one's place at "the table of the gods."

Lord, I have begun to think that it is not possible to be the best kind of politician in the world of today, in which the struggle for power is so all-pervasive.

I'm beginning to think that perhaps the only honest way to engage in politics today is to help men to communicate with each other so that they may discover more and more their true, inalienable personal power and in some way begin to plan their own lives together.

Those who have tasted power and have become hopelessly addicted to it will think that this idea is impossibly utopian.

But for me, here and now, the opposite course is simply genocide.

I have found you, Lord, and I believe in you; and I cannot

forget that you had, in your first small community, the traitor Judas, the professional politician who did not accept and assimilate your new politics.

This was why the influential people of your day chose Judas to sell you out.

It was he who, out of avarice ("He was a thief"), would have prevented the free, creative, generous act of a loving woman with the excuse that the perfume which she was "wasting" on you should have been sold so that the money could have been given to the poor.

You were anything but a professional politician; you sought to free the people and were not interested in power-plays. Hence you showed Judas up for what he was and defended the woman's action.

You were a difficult friend for those who loved power, and you never dreamed of identifying politics with the exercise of power.

You were the first man in history to show the way for a radical change in world politics.

And you did it precisely by renouncing power and by putting yourself at the service of the community, even to the extent of sacrificing your life.

I believe that the best way to begin laying the foundations for the new politics which all the just men on earth have been dreaming about for centuries is to criticize today, as you did yesterday, the political systems of oppression as a matter of conscience.

Lord, who are the ones today who lose their lives for the freedom of their fellowmen—the professional politicians or those who place themselves at the service of man's freedom and progress?

You know the answer.

Lord, give me the strength to carry out my decision, even though some people will spit in my face.

The Worker

Lord,

I am a worker,

a man who is in danger of selling his freedom and his dignity
for a crust of bread.

I am condemned to being a mere object, a robot that goes
through the same motions day after day.

I am the extension of a machine, but even here I am not free
because I am at the service of the machine, which in effect
tells me what to do.

I am no longer a person but only a thing, and as a result I am
continually falling into the temptation to treat other people,
including my wife and children, as so many things too.

I am so tired at the end of my monotonous daily grind that I
can't play peacefully with my children or be a loving
husband to my wife.

When I'm at work I'm a slave, and in my free time I become a
tyrant.

My free time, Lord?

This expression is the clearest proof that we wage earners regard
our working hours as "slave time."

Lord, you were a worker, but you were no slave.

Most often, we have no other alternative: we have to accept

slavery or die of hunger.

Nevertheless, in spite of my lack of education and involvement, I understand quite well that work ought to be something other than slavery.

It ought to be something I accomplish with my hands, something I believe in and put at the service of others.

Lord, I feel that I exist, not to work, but to create, to conceive some project that is useful for men; to plan it with others, if I can't do it alone; to carry it out with my own mind and hands; and to collaborate with others if it is beyond my capabilities.

But nowadays, the worker is never a creator or a planner or even a free agent because everything is imposed on him, and he never has a really effective part to play in any of the initial stages of a project.

The creators, the ones who conceive the ideas, do it for money, and hence come rivalry and competition.

The work that makes slaves of us is programmed by technicians and not by artists or other original thinkers.

We workers have become just blind servants of machinery, and we are punished when we don't obey it.

The system in which we work is degrading and dehumanizing, but even worse, the things we produce militate against men, against ourselves.

I myself produce the very things that are poisoning me and my family.

Could there be any slavery worse than that?

We workers are told that we are in the vanguard of social reform; that we are the ones who are destined to change the face of society and restore justice to the world because we are the most forgotten of all.

But I ask myself how we shall achieve that change since all our energies are primarily devoted to increasing the quantity of poison that we produce.

What real efforts do we make to have society treat us as persons and not as things?

What battles do we fight to a finish to regain our powers of decision?

We are all agreed about working less and earning more, and this is good to the extent that it makes us present a united front to those who, on the contrary, would have us work more and earn less.

But, sad to say, it is not very easy to get us to agree when it is a question of standing up for rights that are much more important and fundamental, for those rights which are really the ones which would allow us to live as persons, free and creative.

For example, how difficult it is for us to get together and plan a new kind of work that would fulfill us, satisfy us and give meaning to our lives!

Lord, when are we going to learn how to see through the wiles of our bosses, who lure us on with the promise of the prosperity which they themselves have attained and which, consciously or unconsciously, we desire for ourselves?

We get angry when the upper classes tell us how well-off we are, because this just seems a pretext which they use to stop us from looking for social and economic justice. But when we examine our consciences, we understand that we shall bring about the real revolution when, without abandoning our fight for economic justice, we strive to appreciate the fact that we are real men and discern our most profound needs, which urge us on to achieve a truly human way of life in justice, freedom and brotherhood, without allowing ourselves to be seduced by false needs and by the illusory sense of power which certain ideologies use as bait.

We have not been made for power.

Instead, we have been made to create the opportunities which will permit men to live a more human life.

And knowing this is our real power.

Therefore, Lord, I realize we can never throw off our chains without a real revolution.

But what kind of revolution?

Should it be a struggle for power, which would simply mean changing one boss for another?

Or should it be the revolution suggested by those who are still living according to the logic of power?

Instead, shouldn't our revolution consist of awakening in our fellow workers the awareness that we must take over that power which has forgotten us and which has prevented us from being real men and from creating a new way of life which will not repeat the old patterns of the past?

Would it be too ingenuous of us to wish to begin again, when we realize that, deep down, we don't like the life-style of our bosses any more than we like our own, because their way of living is also inhuman and degrading.

Don't we workers have the right and the duty to unite and give a common answer to the common needs of all men?

Can we say that such a revolution has ever been seriously considered?

Lord, we workers are not unaware of the special love you have for us.

Hence we'd like to be acutely conscious of our great responsibility as well as of our sacred rights.

I shall continue to ask you for daily bread for my family, and I shall go on struggling to earn it. But I also ask you, Lord, to deliver me every day from the temptation to yearn for middle-class stolidity, because I feel called to be both creative and revolutionary.

Otherwise, we shall be supplanted by the coming generations, in whose eyes we, too, shall appear like accomplices of the forces of exploitation.

In a world which cries out for global revolution, every compromise that is really only a reshuffling of the same elements, and every pact with the exploiters, will be seen as foot-dragging and cowardice.

If all the workers of the world resolutely refused to do work that is slavery and not creativity, they would quickly and radically change this terrible machine which we are daily feeding at the expense of our dignity and our very lives.

Lord, make us workers wake up, because while we go on sleeping, the great revolution will not take place and the world will continue to tug vainly at its chains.

I feel very keenly the call to freedom.

Is this freedom only a dream and not a real possibility?

Yet how can the life that I'm living now be called a reality?

The Scientist

Lord,

my world is the world of matter.

I investigate and delve into things great and small, and I evolve
hypotheses which are beyond the wildest imaginings of the
man in the street.

I have overcome the physical laws that used to ensure the
isolation of the heavenly bodies.

I have discovered the way cells are formed, and I can intervene
to modify their development, so that I am able, at will, to
make supermen or monsters.

I have created new plants and new animals.

I have made it possible to kill everyone on earth simultaneously.

I have grasped the very essence of matter, which is energy, and I
have harnessed and used this energy although I do not
know its nature.

Lord, I recognize that the more I discover, the more there
remains for me to discover, and although I have not yet
been able to do some apparently simple things, such as find
a cure for the common cold, I can see very clearly that
there are no mysteries in the world of matter that will not
ultimately be unravelled by science. Even the death of the
body, which until recently was considered the last frontier
for the scientist, is today just one of many possibilities

within the range of scientific conquest.

But while all these marvellous victories, which sometimes tempt
us to compete with you, are useful enough in themselves,
do they really help to make man's life on earth more free
and more human?

Have I always kept man before my eyes when pursuing my
scientific investigations?

Do I really know man as well as I know matter?

What good will all my science be if it does not begin and end
with man, with his dignity and greatness?

If man is truly the king of creation, science will be science only
when it helps to make man more truly man.

Lord, I must confess that my conquests of matter have not
always been accomplished with man in mind, and this has
been the great shortcoming of my science.

Therefore, I ask you, Lord, to give me a love for man like your
own, for you knew matter better than I ever will, and you
placed it at the service of man whenever it tried to rebel
against him.

Give me this love, because only then shall I be able to cross all
the boundaries of scientific knowledge without fear of going
astray,

and without that keen anguish of having used my scientific
discoveries to destroy life itself.

Lord, I am conscious that my scientific investigation will be an
empty exercise if it is not carried out in the service of man
and if it does not have as its main mission the total
development of the human person instead of the
domination of the few over the many.

If the scientist is to be really at the service of humanity, he must
be a just man;

he must be able to decide when it is worth his while to
conquer new horizons;

he must be able to unite himself with the community and

resist and flee from any alliance with powerful interests that
   could use science, as they usually do whenever possible, to
   destroy men instead of helping them, with the aim of
   holding on to power.

In the past, I have often said that I am a scientist and nothing
   more,
      that I am concerned only with science and that what other
      people do with my discoveries is completely up to them.

But precisely because I am a scientist and because I have some
   power over matter, I have the duty to be concerned about
   the welfare of my fellowmen and about ensuring that
   freedom which will not permit anyone to use for his own
   selfish ends the hard-won victories of the lone scientist.

You see, Lord, that I know very well what an honest scientist
   should be like.

But I need a little more courage so that I will not succumb to
   the subtle temptations that lie in wait for the scientist.

I must not listen to the voice of those lazy people who would
   have me curb my creativity lest I make a false god who
   would compete with you, because I know that it is you who
   have given man the mission of dominating and
   investigating all the marvels of creation.

Nor must I listen to the voice of power that would wish to use
   my science for its own ends.

Science put at the service of self-interest and exploitation would
   be a shameful idolatry;
      a betrayal of man;
      the negation of conscience;
      real atheism.

Lord, although I and many other scientists like me are in very
   close contact with the mysteries of matter, we still do not
   succeed in discovering you and believing in you. Indeed,
   frequently we are professed atheists.

But perhaps our atheism may come from the fact that we have
   closed our eyes to man.

Actually, you never intended matter to be the goal of human
life, as it is in pagan religions, but have always turned our
eyes towards our fellowmen:
"What you did for one of the least of these my brethren, you did
for me."
By forgetting man, the new temple of God, we made it
impossible for us to find you in the heart of matter.

Help us scientists, Lord, to see clearly what our mission ought to
be in the community of men, our brothers.
Make us see that we are living proof to everyone that man can
and should cross all the boundaries of matter in your name;
that effort and creativity are natural to him; and that the
great sin is stagnation.
We must always be at the side of those men who are bringing
about a real revolution, giving them new weapons for the
fight;
we must be the fiercest and most dangerous enemies of
power and exploitation;
we must be the most formidable defenders of the people,
the outcast, the weak, the slaves of this world.
Why do the people, the poor, feel that we are very distant from
them and that we are often the allies of power?
Why don't we go into the marketplace and cry out with the rest
of men that nobody has the right to impose his will on
others and that there exists a real possibility of a happy life
for all and not only for a privileged few?
We often use the excuse that without the help of the powerful
ones of the world, we would not be able to carry on our
scientific work.
But if we were really on the side of the people, wouldn't they be
the first to defend our rights as scientists and consequently
oblige those in power to give us what we need for our work?
Lord, may we never betray the people, because I am convinced
that, if we do, you will despise us.

The Suicide

Lord,
I have tried to commit suicide several times;
I have tried to throw away the greatest gift you gave me, the gift
of life.
I don't know the real reason why I have tried to take my life.
All I know is that I can find no meaning in my existence.
The truth is that life, which everyone says is the most beautiful
thing in the world, is an oppressive burden to me and holds
no joy or even interest for me.
Christ, you did not love death; on the contrary, when you had
been put to death by men, you came back to life as to your
natural element.
Show me what this life you loved so much really is and why it is
worth living in spite of the conditions under which it must
be lived—injustice, absurdity, oppression, loneliness, lies,
domination, slavery, exploitation, silent suffering,
wretchedness, contradiction, and pain of all kinds.
What is this life about which you spoke so often?
Does it consist essentially in being able to plan its course along
with all those who wish to live it seriously?
Or is it the belief that it is possible to overcome all the obstacles
we meet and so make our lives what we feel in the depths
of our hearts they should be?

115

Or does it mean finding some people who are ready to fight every system that takes away man's freedom and doesn't allow him to express himself according to his own originality or to possess the necessities of life which you have provided for all men?

Or does it mean being able to look someone in the eye and feel that he acknowledges and accepts me as a person?

Or is it perhaps the ability to be loved for myself and not for what I have or what I represent?

Or does life mean the possibility of feeling that I am in communion with all men and with everything that exists; that I am truly the lord of all the things you have created and the eventual creator of everything that I love but which I have not yet been able to accomplish?

Does life mean feeling that I am not useless and that everyone expects something of me?

Does it mean finding at least one person who will make me feel that my life is important to her?

However, if this is the life about which you spoke, I have never known it, nor have I ever done anything to know it.

I have always found that I am useless to myself and to everyone else.

No one has ever had any faith in me, and I have never had any faith in anyone.

I have found no one who was ready to struggle side by side with me, nor have I ever offered to fight along with others in widening the field of man's freedom.

Nobody has ever loved me.

Everyone has used me.

And I have used others when I could.

No one has ever looked me in the eye so that he could get to know me and allow me to know him.

In fact, I have done everything possible to hide my deepest needs from myself and from everyone else.

I have never given anything to anyone because I was afraid of losing myself, yet little by little I became so empty there were no longer any boundaries between me and nothingness.

I have never felt that I was united with other men.

I have never recognized the fact that everything that exists around me was created for me.

Not only did I not know how to gather up your gift of life, but I even amused myself by destroying it.

I have justified all the ugliness that I have found within me by saying that I didn't feel loved.

But I understand now, Lord, that it was I who did not love, for it was I who felt the lack of love; it was I who felt the need to be loved and the possibility of loving in return.

Why haven't I had hope, Lord?

Why have I chosen self-destruction as the goal of my life?

What fear led me to choose death, the thing that is most hateful to man's nature?

Although I don't see the answer clearly, Lord, I feel that today something has been born deep within me which is quite different from despair,

something which urges me on to risk accepting life as you did.

I don't know yet how I shall do it, but I know that you found meaning in life.

Yet no one knew the ugliness and injustice of men as you did.

But not only did you not despair of life by committing suicide: you believed in life so deeply that you generously sacrificed your own life so that we might be able to find meaning in ours.

I cannot forget, Lord, that I have tried to do away with myself, and that at the very moment at which you were shamefully condemned to death for defending life, one of your friends and apostles was committing suicide out of bitter regret at having betrayed Life itself.

Yet it is you and not Judas who are the universal symbol of hope in, and love for, that life about which every man dreams.

Lord, make me understand that men will not discover what is good and infinite in life by a cowardly refusal to fight for it but rather by believing in it so deeply, although without understanding it completely, that they will be ready to lose it in defending it.

Only thus, after having lost one's own life for the sake of others, is there a hope of a more vivid life which no one can.lose or would ever want to lose, because it will be the total revelation of man's reason for existence.

Lord, I, a would-be suicide, want to cry out to all those like me in the world that nothing can justify the taking of our lives.

Now I understand that it was only fear of life that impelled me to choose death.

I must realize, Lord, that I cannot hope or pretend that it is others who provide me with a reason for going on living.

It is not others who must build my life for me.

I must build for myself a life that is worth living.

I shall build it in the company of those who have discovered that life, and not death, is man's natural dimension.

In future, Lord, let me not confuse my inability to fight with a mad gesture of self-destruction.

Make me feel responsible for the lives of others so that I may have less time to think about myself.

The Doctor

Lord,

I am a doctor.

Every day I deal with the masterpiece of your creation, the human body.

Before telling you my worries and the contradictions involved in the exercise of my profession, I beg you to teach me always to regard man's body as the most fantastic spectacle in creation.

May I always remember, Lord, that you yourself looked upon it with admiration and joy when you had created it.

And may I never forget that man's body, as well as his soul, has been made in your "image and likeness."

Christ, you were the first real doctor in history, because no one felt as angry and distressed as you did when confronted by anything that harmed the human body.

Your great love of life impelled you to cure any sick person you met.

You have been the only doctor in history who cured everyone.

Make me understand, Lord, the secret that made you intolerant of any kind of sickness.

What is so great and so mysterious about the human body that, when you decided to remain among men in the Eucharist, you did so not only spiritually but also corporally?

In your eyes, curing a man of an illness was more important than fulfilling the letter of the law.

But what about me?

I must confess, Lord, that often I don't practice my profession as I should but exploit it to get rich.

I cash in on the fact that my profession has no competition to fear because it deals with man's very life.

Lord, how many people have beggared themselves seeking a cure?

I'm ashamed to admit that we doctors often regard a rich man's body as being more important than a poor man's.

Why else do we run so much more quickly to the bedside of a rich or powerful man than we do to that of someone who has neither money nor fame?

We always examine a rich patient with meticulous care, while we generally do little more for a poor one than fill in a form and send him off to the hospital.

And what is even worse and more shameful, we sometimes stoop so low as to use men's natural love of life by diagnosing sicknesses that they do not have in order to make money by performing needless surgery.

We play games with the most sacred thing on earth.

And what about medicines, Lord?

Every time I prescribe a medicine, am I convinced of its effectiveness, or am I, too, guilty of contributing to the horrible commercial trafficking in medicines that is widely promoted by advertisements?

Unhappily, Lord, we doctors, too, pay tribute to a society that uses man in every way possible instead of placing itself unreservedly at his service.

Sometimes we feel that we are powerless to save lives or alleviate suffering because society, instead of dedicating its riches to serve science on man's behalf, uses those riches to harm or even kill him.

Yet I do realize, Lord, that this does not justify my doing

nothing.

Who should be more insistent than a doctor in reminding society of its injustice and waste?

We doctors are more responsible than anyone else for not rebelling against the waste involved in manufacturing arms and needless luxuries because we are closest to, and feel most powerless against, man's pain, suffering and death.

Our specific mission should be the defense of man's health and life against the adulteration of food, the contamination of the environment, and chemical products that, under the pretext of curing, often impair health.

We should band together and make society use for the benefit of man the countless billions it devotes to his destruction.

Everything that man today uses to destroy himself should be put in our hands, not only to cure the ills that afflict and often kill him, but also to enable us to seek out new ways of life more suited to man and his complete liberation.

Lord, if we are unable to wage this war and if we go on regarding medicine mainly as a way to get rich, we ought at least have the courage to admit that we are not healers but murderers, because our first responsibility is our fellowmen's physical health and life, which are the prime requirements for their existence as men and as persons.

It is true that I do not have at my disposal all the means necessary for finding the origin of, and cure for, all the ills that afflict man.

Yet if I treat each patient with more love and attention, I shall discover that the majority of the ills that afflict man are the result of social injustice, inhuman working conditions, poverty, ignorance and the increasingly impossible circumstances in which he is compelled to live.

Let me not forget, Lord, that the human body is not a machine and that, consequently, I cannot cure its ailments merely by examining it physically or treating it chemically.

If a doctor is faithful to his mission of healing, no one

understands better than he that every illness is closely connected with the total mystery of man.

It is not possible to cure a body while forgetting that it belongs to a person, to a marvellous complex of body and soul which thinks and loves.

If a doctor does not take into account the whole person, body *and* soul, he is not a physician but a mechanic.

Yet, Lord, this does not mean that I am against specialization.

There are great advantages for medicine in specialization, which allows individual doctors to deepen their knowledge of particular diseases or parts of the body.

But we should do so as part of a team.

If we don't, we reduce man to the level of a machine, and each of us concentrates on one gear or cog or process, while no one is responsible for the correct functioning of the whole.

And still people will go on paying tribute to our profession, not realizing that whatever does not serve for the total, concrete benefit of men is immoral and sinful, although they know full well that, while Pilate did wash his hands in public, he did not thereby rid himself of the sin of deicide in the eyes of history.

Christ, may we doctors have the courage and the joy of recognizing that we are the new wonder-workers of history because you have confided to us the task of continuing the permanent miracle of keeping life alive.

May we regard our responsibility to humanity as a pleasure and not as a burden.

And let us not forget that there is no limit to our possibilities because, since you conquered death, man has the right to fight against all his physical limitations.

If that were not so, any gesture that medicine made to develop or sustain man's life on earth would be immoral, as would have been your miracles which prolonged life and abolished pain.

The fact that you never tolerated sickness or death in others shows us clearly that these limitations are not normal to man, but are only the result of a collective sin which you came to remedy once and for all.

You told us yourself that we will be able to do greater things than you did.

And *you* raised the dead!

Lord, may I treat every patient I attend with the care, gentleness and generosity that I would like to see lavished upon me when I am ill myself.

Perhaps I, as a doctor, can understand better than others what you meant when you said: "Love your neighbor as yourself."

The Priest

Lord, what is a priest?

For some people, he is a selfish solitary, while others regard him
   as an uninteresting bachelor, or a religious bureaucrat.

Some say that he is a gift of God, one who loves his fellowmen
   more than anyone else does.

Some bless him, while others pity him.

And many simply ignore him.

Almost nobody knows what a priest is.

I wonder, Lord, do I myself know?

There are some who do not yet realize that a priest, too, can
   betray them; that they ought not to trust him because of the
   mere fact that he is a priest.

Yesterday the priesthood was a privilege, and at the lowest, a
   good job.

But today it is often a challenge and a risk.

Nowadays many people can't understand a priest apart from his
   people, his community, his work.

They don't understand a priest who does not love this earth,
   who has no friends and who isn't just another man among
   men.

The priest exists for the community and only for the
   community.

But not everyone in a community thinks the same way, Lord.

Therefore it is difficult to be a priest.

The poor are angry if he associates with the rich, and they call him a capitalist.

And the rich are insulted if he is true to the Gospel and devotes himself to the poor, and they call him a communist.

The pious fear for his interior life if at times he cuts short his prayers to help someone in need.

And the worldly-minded look at him pityingly when they see him kneeling before the tabernacle.

If his celibacy seems to bring him joy and freedom, and if he states emphatically that he doesn't feel any more lonely than his married friends, people suspect his chastity.

If he locks himself up in solitude and is at great pains to protect his virtue, they will accuse him of escapism and "angelism."

What *is* a priest, Lord?

If he dresses poorly, he is an agitator.

If he dresses well, he is a middle-class snob.

If he is a pastor of souls, he is accused of theological fuzziness.

If he is an intellectual, people will say that he lacks the common touch.

If he is happy, enjoys life and believes in love, he is "worldly" and not a "churchman."

If he lives an austere, ascetic life, they will say that he is a "monk" and not a "committed" priest of the twentieth century.

If he does not condemn revolution or if he joins others in calling for justice, he is being false to the Beatitude: "Blessed are the peacemakers . . ."

If he preaches peace and nonviolence, he is betraying the Christ of the oppressed, who came "to bring, not peace, but the sword," and he arouses the anger of the poor and the outcasts who have lost patience and are tired of waiting.

If he obeys the Church, he is part of the system.

If he opens up new paths by rebelling against many things in
which he no longer believes, he is a progressive.

To whom should he listen, Lord?

To one side or the other?

To everyone?

To no one?

Should he listen to those who are still scandalized by John the
Baptist because he lived in the desert, went about half-
naked and starved himself, or to those who haven't yet got
over the fact that the Son of Man went to banquets and
chatted with sinners and prostitutes?

Is it true that the priest's one, real role is to be a sign of
contradiction?

But if this is so, Lord, compromise and diplomacy will never
lead to the scandal of the cross,
and much less to a yearning for the resurrection.

The Civil Servant

Lord,
I am just a minor civil servant.
There are millions of us in the world, and we know that it
would be difficult to find a more boring, uncreative and
unappreciated job.
Then why do we do it?
Simply to earn a living for ourselves and our families.
Lord, I don't think that anyone has a vocation to be a "civil
servant." Our work is just one of the many forms of slavery
that have been created by a society that has to defend its
structures at all costs.
Our job exists because a bureaucracy exists which has, in fact,
turned into a hidden tyranny.
Bureaucracy is a power which has taken advantage of man's
lack of responsibility to justify its whole machinery, without
which, at this stage, there would be chaos.
Our work is not only boring and uncreative, it is also poorly
paid.
We earn less than most skilled or semi-skilled manual workers.
Granted that the immature world of today needs a certain
amount of bureaucracy, and granted also that somebody
has to do the paperwork, which stunts instead of maturing
him and awakening his creativity, why isn't the minor civil

servant paid at least a decent wage so that he may have a margin of possibility to develop himself in other fields of creative work?

Even worse, our humiliation is still greater because we feel that we are slaves to our bosses, who are not always the most intelligent of men and many of whom got their jobs as a result of political or economic influence.

We have to do work for them which we know could be done much better another way, but the ordinary civil servant is not allowed the least initiative where his boss is concerned.

Worse still, the bosses themselves are the very ones who are most interested in seeing to it that we are not creative, because they don't want to risk the danger of having a minor official showing that he is smarter than they are.

And if, occasionally, our creativity does come to the surface and is accepted because it is too evident and too valuable to be suppressed, it will never be presented as ours and will be used only as a feather in the boss's cap.

In our job, teamwork is very reluctantly accepted because it would weaken the power-structure and would leave room only for an authority that is born of competence and the force of truth.

Lord, our work has the further humiliation of not being recognized or appreciated, either by those who tell us what to do or by those for whom we do it.

Today a manual worker has his own dignity as a member of the work-force of the nation.

He, at least, makes something, cars or kitchens.

But what do we make?

At best, we are seen as people who make others lose an awful lot of time.

The manual worker has the satisfaction of being able to look at the product of his work, even though the things he produces are made for others.

But all we do is protect other people's power.

They try to console us by telling us that we are rendering a great
service to the community.

But I wonder if this is true?

I would willingly accept rendering a service to help a man who,
in his turn, is also serving others; by relieving him of some
of his work-load, I would be collaborating with him in the
liberation of all men.

But in reality, most of us civil servants are serving a power-
machine that brushes men to one side, or we are working
for certain people who are not by any means serving others
but who devote themselves to serving money, ideologies or
their own prestige.

Working for someone who doesn't have enough time to serve
others personally as much as he would like can be
dignified and worthwhile.

But working for someone who has no time to serve anyone but
himself and his own interests is slavery and degradation.

Lord, is there any chance for us minor civil servants to revolt, to
wake up to our dignity as men and to our possibility to be
creative within the present dehumanizing system?

Lord, this is my simple but urgent prayer today:
    may we never lose hope of being able to put our shoulder to
    the wheel of liberation that is now turning in all sections of
    labor.

I know that this is not easy to do, but I don't want to despair.

It is not easy because the machine in which we are caught up is
both powerful and merciless.

Standing behind his little window, the civil servant is quite
aware that people must come to him to ask for the little
pieces of official paper that will authorize them to obtain
something that is already a fundamental right of life.

And therefore, he asks himself, sometimes very angrily, why it is
necessary for people to have those pieces of paper.

But then he reflects that, without the pieces of paper, they
couldn't go on living.

Yet, worst of all, Lord, the civil servant may fall into a grave temptation;

he may take out his frustration on those he serves.

Feeling that he is condemned to being a machine that dispenses pieces of paper in the name of power, he may become so harsh and embittered that he will regard those who come to him, not as human persons, but as machines like himself.

His inability to be creative may bring him to deny others that possibility in their turn, and, instead of trying to lessen or eliminate the burden of bureaucracy for those who approach him, sometimes he himself deliberately increases that burden and makes it even more hateful than it has to be, thus taking secret, and often unconscious, revenge for his own enslavement.

Yes, Lord, we civil servants, who suffer more than anybody else the tragic consequences of the inhumanity of bureaucracy, should be its greatest enemies.

We should develop our creativeness precisely in order to study how to simplify as much as possible this common slavery.

If a revolution against bureaucracy is possible, we are the ones most responsible and most prepared for seeing that it comes as quickly as possible.

We are the ones who must fight, actively or passively, to simplify the ordinary man's relationships with the power-structures and to have his fundamental rights granted directly to him and not through a long line of minor officials.

If we are able to undertake this revolution, we shall show that our creative capacity has not been completely destroyed.

And perhaps at this moment of history, no other kind of creativeness may be more useful and more liberating for humanity, since bureaucracy is one of the most subtle and most stultifying forms of modern slavery, one that has evident repercussions on the creativeness of all men.

I believe that it would be one of the gravest sins today to resign ourselves to our jobs as minor civil servants and to the loss of our creativity.

Since we regard our work as enslavement and not as a vocation, our first cry of protest ought to be to ask ourselves if it is just that some men should be born to be civil servants by the mere fact that they can find no other way to make a living.

Lord, is it just that there should be some men who have no choice but to be civil servants?

If power were shared by all, the minor civil servant's function of acting as a cushion between the powers that be and the ordinary citizen would not be needed.

And the minimum of bureaucracy, which perhaps will always be required, could very well be a service rendered by everyone in turn.

Lord, the very world that exploits us regards us with pity or indifference and does not believe in our revolutionary possibilities.

But will you, at least, Lord, look at us with dignity, and not lose hope in out ability to free ourselves?

You, Christ, were the fiercest opponent of the useless laws that enslaved the people of your time, and you were harshly punished for not observing them.

The Personnel Manager

Lord,
before I start praying to you,
I want to warn you that I am a strange character, one of
the black sheep of the world of employment.
I am a personnel manager,
a watchdog in a white collar.
And people are right to have this opinion of me.
The owners of firms and factories invented the job of personnel
   manager so that they could use to the best possible
   advantage a raw material which was quite cheap but
   difficult to "handle"—human labor.

Although the world of human labor belongs so completely to
   you, since everything human is yours through the
   Incarnation and since labor is yours through creation,
   Satan is not far from it.
And man has become a prey that is being fought over by those
   in power.
Their methods have become more refined with time, but the
   ordinary man is still victimized.
The scientific organization of labor has now been replaced by
   so-called "human relations," but the personnel manager's
   job remains the same, even when he is made an executive,

as in the larger firms.

But, as you know, Lord, love and respect for neighbor can blossom even in the heart of a bandit.

Therefore, I am sure that you will listen to my prayer.

You know that it is sincere.

You know that even I need to cry out to you my pain and anguish of conscience.

A lot of people wouldn't understand my feelings.

If I told them, they would simply laugh at me because no one thinks that a personnel manager would get down on his knees to pray earnestly to you, the lover of humanity and of human values.

In fact, many people believe that we personnel managers don't even have souls.

Lord, I am torn by the conflict between being a servant of my bosses and a true friend to the weak and oppressed.

I know that the workers are my brothers whom I must help to fulfill themselves, and not so many cogs in the machinery of production, to be oiled or replaced.

My father was one of those cogs, and I am still suffering from the burden he had to bear and the tribute he had to pay.

Therefore, Lord, help me to preserve and increase my sensitivity to human values.

Help me to recognize you in every worker, especially in those who are regarded as "black sheep" because they have been pushed to the fringes of the system or even outside it, or because they have bravely devoted themselves to defending the rights of their companions.

May I never refuse to help someone who is looking for a job by taking refuge in the cold, inexorable logic of selection techniques.

May I always remember that production must be for man and not man for production.

Christ, give me the strength to resist the violence of those influential people who, in their never-ending wheeling and dealing, often try to force their proteges on me, with no regard for the most elementary demands of justice.

Help me to help those who have no "pull"; those who can repay me with nothing more than a surprised "Thank you!"

But isn't it just at such moments that I'll see how even my work can bring me closer to you?

Lord, save me from the gratitude of influential people, which would tangle me up in a web of favors and obligations from which it would be difficult to free myself.

With us, too, they use the tactics of "the stick and the carrot."

When everybody is looking for success, money and security, it is very hard to resist the temptation to sell out one's conscience for the glittering prizes with which industry rewards cowardice and conformity.

Nevertheless, help me to see all men as my neighbors, including even those proteges of the bosses, whom I instinctively dislike.

Help me to respect these people's authentic rights and human dignity in spite of the "recommendations" they enjoy.

Give me the words to convince them that, without justice, there is no joy or self-improvement for anyone.

Besides, Lord, many of them have done nothing except having to get a job and earn a living.

They were brought up to believe in string-pulling and in the motto: "It's not what you know, but *who* you know!"

And so it is not surprising that they curry favor with influential people, not to cheat anyone, but to get fair treatment for themselves, as they conceive it.

Lord, I also ask you to help me have the strength to oppose as well as I can, and even at the risk of my job, the exploitation of men in their work, especially when this exploitation is done with the "consent" of the workers.

You know how difficult it is to protect the physical, psychological and moral integrity of those who work in a commercial concern, when the bosses offer money as compensation for the "inevitable" injuries which the system of production causes to the workers.

Fortunately, the workers themselves have begun to wake up to their game.

May I not allow a man to be judged by his accuser, or be prevented from defending himself or from making a swift and timely appeal against judges whom he considers unjust.

Help me, Lord, to be strong, for you have been the best witness to, and defender of, every human value.

Free me also from the most subtle and diabolical danger that I have to face— that of neo-capitalist paternalism, of which I may at any moment become the unwilling instrument.

In a society in which the citizen still lacks many of the means that would enable him to obtain those rights which are his by law, industry is inclined to take the place of the state so that it can make the workers increasingly dependent on it for "fringe benefits."

Help me to be constantly alert in ensuring that the worker will not be corrupted by anything he receives from the bosses.

Help me to make sure that the whole concept of favors, assistance and generosity on the part of management will be replaced by the idea of justice and the worker's rights.

Help me to believe and hope that the day is not far off when the civic community, and not commercial interests, will direct all the services that everyone needs, for physical and mental health, education, housing, loans, insurance and the like.

Help me also, Lord, to bear witness to our obligation of love for our neighbor in labor relations with my fellow workers.

May I never be one of those who preaches but doesn't practice, who says he wants to protect man's dignity in work and who then practices authoritarianism and paternalism in his own job.

Help me to make sure that my actions are in accordance with

my principles by examining my conscience and by really listening to those who have the right and the duty to judge the validity of my decisions—
the workers, the trade unions and the members of the Christian community of which I am a part.

Lord, I understand that, even if I achieve everything I have talked to you about, I shall do little more than make less burdensome the lot of the workers in our firm.

You are the only real teacher of liberty and the only true revolutionary in history; and therefore you know that, if men are to find in their work the principal means of genuine development and creativity, it will be necessary to revolutionize the whole make-up and all the objectives, not only of our firm, but of the entire social system.

Lord, I don't know how much I, working within the system, can contribute by way of effort and ideas to bring about the great change, the humanization of work and society.

But I feel the responsibility that you have given to everyone to use the talents you have bestowed on him and to do so without being afraid to risk them.

Yet I don't want to risk anyone's hide but my own.

Lord, at least never let it happen that through fear or confusion of ideas, I should end up by helping to oppress my fellowmen. Like the blind men you met while you were on earth, I cry out:

Lord, that I may see!

Those Who Don't Like the Other Form of Prostitution

Lord, you have said that we are not to fear those who can kill our bodies,

but rather those who can kill our souls.

Consequently, isn't it worse to sell one's soul than to sell one's body?

Why, then, do we despise those who sell their bodies for a few coins to buy food, while we respect so many of those who sell their own souls and those of their innocent victims?

No one would dare to introduce a professional prostitute into polite society, yet no one is ashamed of introducing people whom we know to be selling out the truth.

Of course, it is not right to sell one's body, because the body is the Creator's gift and the earthly abode of love.

But selling the soul is worse.

Yet who is ashamed of, or worried about, those who publicly sell their souls?

Very properly, the Catholic press is scandalized at, and raises its voice against, the flood of pornography, that black market of the human body.

But when will these same newspapers cry out against those who sell millions of children into virtual slavery, thus sacrificing their budding lives on the altar of consumerism?

Or against those who try to take the Creator's place by changing

the purpose of creation, which is to put things at the service
of man, and not the other way around?

Or against those who abuse the truth by denying it, hiding it,
falsifying it, selling it, prostituting it?

Isn't it more diabolical to sell out the truth than to sell one's
body?

Who will cry out against the prostitution and the pornography of
the truth?

Who will cry out against those who every day sell off the last
tatters of peace and hope remaining to the oppressed, to
those who cannot avail themselves of the press and
television to let the world know of the injustices they have
to suffer?

Who will denounce those who call peace "war," and war
"peace"?

Those who call chains "freedom," and freedom "slavery"?

Those who call oppression "justice," and justice "revolution"?

Those who call the use of human beings as chattels "love," and
who call love for justice "hate"?

Lord, who will cry out against those who sell out the truth of
your Gospel, obscuring and denying it at the very table of
the people of God who are awaiting their liberation?

No one is afraid of him who sells out the truth.

No one is ashamed of shaking his hand or contracting his
leprosy.

We think that we are clean when we don't put our bodies, our
reputations or our morality up for sale, but do we ever
seriously examine our consciences about the underhand
trafficking in truth that we are continually engaged in?

It is true that not all of us have cause to be ashamed or repent of
having ever prostituted our bodies, but how many of us can
stand up and swear that we haven't prostituted the truth?

Hence, Lord, we are not ashamed or afraid of the hucksters of
truth because we are all accomplices, to some degree, in

that terrible conspiracy that tries to exclude you from history so that it can change your truth into its own version.

Lord, while we are becoming more aware of the sinfulness of our spiritual prostitution, let us at least be less severe in throwing the first stone at those who engage in the prostitution of the body.

Let us not use them as decoys to distract attention from our own sin, which is more shameful and more dangerous.

When you said: "The harlots will go before you into the kingdom of heaven," you meant to do much more than show that you understand and have compassion on the weaknesses of the flesh.

These words of yours were a cry of alarm against that other, more subtle and more diabolical form of prostitution, which is capable of putting up for sale truth itself, which is you, and of selling it, too, for money or a shoddy bit of power.

That was the sin of those who gave you over to death, smothering the truth, to gain possession of its throne.

From fear of these hucksters, do *not* deliver us, Lord.

The Journalist

Lord,

we are journalists.

We are coming to pray to you together because we know that everyone else, without exception, casts stones at us.

Everyone needs us, but they all condemn us.

Everyone seeks us out, but later they all criticize us.

Today the world would be paralyzed without us, yet most people would cheerfully hang us.

We are not coming to you to make excuses for our limitations or gloss over our sins.

We admit to having both limitations and sins.

And we are aware that we have the grave responsibility of sharing the intimate secrets of others every day, of sitting down at all the tables of the world, and of knowing that the vast majority of people form their opinions from what we say.

Yet we too must cry out about our need for justice.

Lord, are we worse than those who condemn us?

Than those who use us?

Than those who complain, not so much that we prostitute our talents, but rather that we don't do so in the direction they'd like?

Often many influential people would prefer us to keep quiet; but it is our duty to let everyone know what's going on. Others would prefer us to write only about pleasant things that wouldn't disturb their sleep or their digestions, but we must speak in the name of those who cannot speak for themselves, of those who are not free, of those who are suffering in their very flesh the reality of the news that disturbs us.

And isn't it much more painful to suffer something than merely to hear about it?

Yet when we report unpleasant things, people call it "sensationalism," but it could also be called "human suffering that we would like to forget about."

Lord, we find it much easier to speak to you than to outsiders because we know that you were the first great newspaperman in history.

You are the Word who became flesh and made the greatest news men have ever heard:

God became man so that man would lose his fear of being God.

You told your followers to become journalists and announce the truth "from the housetops."

You were always the journalist of the people, of all those who were persecuted by injustice or tyranny.

When you wrote or spoke, it was always to save that which was lost, to condemn those who were trying to take over man and his history in the name of God or Caesar.

The only time you wrote with your own hand, you wrote on the ground to save the life of a woman taken in adultery.

You were the first journalist to be censored by your own Church, since this incident of the adultress was, for a long time, omitted from the majority of ancient manuscripts of the Gospels "lest it give rise to abuses."

This means that you were accused of being imprudent and over-generous!

Actually, you were the first journalist to be
scandalous,

critical,
revolutionary,
nonconformist,
and sincere!
And so they said that you were possessed by the devil,
    that you were an atheist,
    and they pelted you with stones and finally killed you while
    you were still a young man.
You had to work miracles to get your news believed, and still a
    lot of people refused to believe in you despite your miracles.
Perhaps we poor newspapermen can take comfort from all this,
    for not only are we unable to back up our news with
    miracles, but we sometimes need a miracle worked for us to
    get people to forgive us when we uncover a morsel of truth,
    especially when the truth is bitter for those who have taken
    over history and pushed the weak to one side.

Lord, we can say it frankly to you.
It's not easy to be a journalist.
It's not easy to be honest, because we would need some of your
    heroism to go on risking our lives and livelihood.
It's not easy, because we get our daily bread and that of our
    families precisely from those who are most interested in
    preventing the world from hearing the bald truth about
    things.
It's not easy, because those who need and want to know the
    whole truth about things cannot help us to tell it.
It's not easy, because if we talk about the shameful things of the
    world, we are pessimists, while if we speak about the
    hidden virtues of good men, we are escapists.
If we talk about God, we're "holy Joes," while if we talk about
    man, we're Communists.
If we talk about the future, we're progressives, and if we talk
    about the past, we're reactionaries, while if we speak about
    the present, we're unthinking.

We're expected to be honest, although every day we hear the sordid details of dirty deals.

We're expected to be incorruptible, although every day we have to keep silent about the corrupt practices of so many people.

We're expected to be untainted, although every day we are made aware of the many types of prostitution practiced by "respectable" crooks whom we are often forced to praise in print.

We're expected to be accurate and truthful, although we often have to elbow our way in to get news or report a speech.

We're expected to do a write-up on the novena to St. Anne, while priests are out demonstrating in the streets and the world is asking itself if God hasn't died.

We're resented when we leave out a paragraph from a speech by a politician or a churchman extolling the glories of the past, while we don't even have the time or the space to cry out the evils of the present.

We are asked to publish the pastorals of bishops for whom the clock of history has stopped, while we should be preaching the revolutionary words of a Christ whom we have not yet had the courage to quote in full, or while we should be reporting the prophetic words of the people of God telling us that the Holy Spirit is not dead.

Lord, everyone seeks us out because they need us— the politicians need us to vouch for them; the religionists need us to spread their teachings; the industrialists need us to sell their wares; the scientists need us to make their findings known; the artists need us to let everybody know about their work; and the people need us to defend them.

Yet they all curse us and pelt us with stones—the politician, when we denounce his rabble-rousing or betrayal of trust; the churchman, when we show up his pharisaism;

the industrialist, when we blow the whistle on his profiteering;

the scientist, when we reveal the unworthy use he makes of

his discoveries;

the artist, when we point out his lack of originality;

and the people, when we don't have the courage to object loudly enough to suit them, although they speak so little on their own behalf that they have lost their voices.

Perhaps we newspapermen find it easier to pray than anyone else because we are closer to life and all its contradictions; because we know people as few others do; because every day we see at close quarters the crying need for more justice in the world.

Forgive us, Lord, for the times we betray the truth through cowardice or self-interest.

Forgive us for our spineless kowtowing to influential people who don't like to hear the truth.

In fact, there is only one thing that we cannot ask your forgiveness for, only one sin of which we cannot repent, because, if it is a sin, you have committed it, too—and that is the sin of having angered influential people by revealing the dirty games they play in manipulating the lives of the poor and the weak, who are unable to defend themselves.

May we never lose hope or be ashamed of being the voice crying in the wilderness, because one day that wilderness may be the land inhabited by the pure of heart.

Those Who Are Afraid of Anything New

Lord, why do we feel safer with the past than with the future?

Why do we find it almost physically painful to bid goodbye to the old year when we know that a new one awaits us?

Why do we have that feeling of let-down, loss and even death when, in reality, we are ascending, arriving and coming to life?

At the end of the year, we say sadly that we have one year "less," as if the goal of life were behind us, as if, with each passing year, we are leaving our dearest friend farther and farther behind as we move away from him.

But, Lord, aren't things really quite the opposite?

Aren't you coming to meet us?

Aren't we getting closer and closer to happiness?

With every year that passes, we are not being swept farther away from what we love, but are coming ever closer to it.

As we grow older, our faces should increasingly reflect the joy that is awaiting us.

Why then do we look sadder, more hardened and more bitter with each passing year?

Does death weigh us down more than life buoys us up?

Can't we bring ourselves to believe that dawn is more promising than nightfall?

Are not unbelievers often the very ones who believe this most realistically and most productively?

Don't we find it hard to accept that you never lag behind but are always waiting for us up ahead?

Shouldn't you signify for us everything that we are desperately wishing and searching for?

When we are born and come out into the light of day, we cry and suffer more than when we were enclosed in the darkness of the womb.

Our life begins to unfold, but in spite of finding you, we continue to live in bondage to our human needs and to be incapable of being born anew to a different mode of life.

And like unthinking infants, we tremble at every new light, at every new current of air, at every new face.

We are more afraid of what is born in us than of what dies in us.

Lord, we are unable to believe that you are more in that which is beginning than in that which is ending, more in that which is coming than in that which no longer exists, for you do not repeat yourself, Lord, and you are always revealing yourself more and more.

We are unable to admit that, precisely because you never repeat yourself, we cannot sanctify as "unique" anything from the past.

We are unable to appreciate fully the fact that you never make two days the same, two faces exactly alike, two identical loves, two interchangeable life stories, two indistinguishable blades of grass.

We cannot believe that you are continually coming closer to us.

And so we rarely feel your presence in what's new. What is the source of this sadness at the passage of time, this bitterness because the years are gliding by?

When shall we be able to cry out with faith that we are genuinely better today than we were yesterday; that each tick of the clock assures us that we can improve still more;

and that we can beget in ourselves something new,
different,
surprising,
and unexpected
at every bend in the road?
Lord, if we really believe in you,
in ourselves,
and in other men,
then, instead of bemoaning the death of each year, we would be tempted to put forward the hands of the clock.
An artist can repeat himself and can fall short of his best efforts.
But you never repeat yourself and always improve on what you have done.
Yet you are living within us, and something in our hearts tells us so.
Lord, didn't you yourself say to us: "You shall do greater things than I have done"?
Shall we ever have sufficient faith in ourselves to believe that we are really capable of not repeating ourselves and of continually outdoing our best achievements?

The Condemned Man

I have been condemned to death,
as you were, Lord, although you were innocent.
I'm not innocent, not by a long shot!
But, then, who is?
If only the innocent were allowed to live, the whole world would
    suddenly become one big cemetery.
You, who were yourself condemned to death, were always
    against capital punishment.
If you hadn't intervened, the adulterous woman would have
    been battered to death under a hail of rocks.
Every time someone wants to assume power over another man's
    life, you'd like some innocent person to confront him and
    say:
"Let him who is without sin be the first to cast a stone, to pull
    the trigger, to throw the switch!"
It's not a question of innocence or guilt: the adulterous woman
    was certainly guilty, for she was caught in the act.
Rather is it a matter of one man's right to take away another
    man's life.
I am speaking from the death cell, as you know, Lord, and no
    doubt this does influence my point of view.
But I cannot help thinking that every time we men take the life
    of a fellow human being in the name of any right

whatsoever, we are committing the greatest sin against mankind, because we are usurping the place of God, who is the only lord of man's life.

We really don't make the lives and rights of some men more secure by slaughtering others.

Just as violence breeds violence, death can only breed death, and we can overcome death only by a superabundance of life.

Everything else is venting our anger, revenge, the projection of our unconscious masochism, a parody of justice.

Even when your murderers were crucifying you, they said that they were doing it to ensure that justice was carried out and the will of the people enforced.

They were all convinced that you were a danger to the security of the system!

When someone is put to death in the name of justice of one kind or another, perhaps there is one criminal less in the world, but there certainly is one sinner less to repent and possibly become a good citizen.

The creative work of God, which He has entrusted to man, is not done by smothering injustice with death, but by overcoming it by love, that creative love which is capable of making sons of Abraham out of the very stones.

Every time society helps a criminal to reform, it raises a man from the dead, while every time society kills a man, it repeats the crucifixion of Christ.

You were the most innocent man the world has ever seen, yet you were condemned to death by a human tribunal.

Isn't this the best proof that human justice is fragile and fallible?

That terrible miscarriage of our justice should have been enough to have abolished the death penalty, at least among those who honor your name.

Only those who have not yet discovered the full dignity of man are capable of upholding capital punishment, which is the last relic of civic cannibalism.

I love life so much that I am clinging to the hope of a last-minute reprieve; yet I can see how others in my position may regard themselves as already dead once sentence has been passed, and I can also understand how others, with supreme heroism, neither ask for nor accept mercy, but die, as you did, with a cry of protest against injustice, a cry of love for the great gift of life.

Lord, I am a condemned man, and it matters little whether I'm awaiting death in Europe, America, Africa or Asia.

Tyranny and injustice have the same face everywhere, the face of someone who does not recognize the other man's dignity and his inalienable right to life.

Lord, I'm sitting here waiting for them to come and put an end to my earthly existence.

But who are "they"?

They're not the judges,
> nor the magistrates,
> nor the heads of state,
> all those who, with a stroke of the pen, have made possible this new sin.

I know that they wouldn't be able to come and pull the trigger or throw the switch themselves.

Yet while these new Pilates, Herods and Caiaphases hide in the shadows, and while the populace cry out: "Kill him!", I shall be executed by men who really don't want to do it because I never harmed them.

Lord, isn't this symbolic of humanity's most tragic failing, man's haste to unload on someone else his own responsibility?

The authorities signed my death sentence without qualms because they knew that they wouldn't have to carry it out in person; and the executioners will do their grisly job, also without qualms, because they consider that the orders they receive from higher authority render them guiltless.

And I am to die because I can't make them understand how absurd the whole thing is!

Lord, I do not desire, much less accept, my death, but must

submit to being killed.

Yet I do not want to go to my death like a coward, kicking and screaming, or like an unfeeling stoic.

I do not accept my death, even though, in a moment of insanity, I did take another man's life, because I feel that we have been created for life and not for death.

But since I must die, I shall do so sorrowfully, yet not in despair, so that I can make people understand that no one can kill me or anyone else once and for all, because we are greater than death itself.

I'd like my unwilling death to be a great shout for life,
　　just as your death on the cross was,
　　to shake the earth,
　　make men ashamed,
　　and wake the dead from their tombs.

Now I see that we are dead only when we do not understand the value of life, even that of the worst criminal.

Therefore, although I am on the brink of the grave, I feel that I am very much alive, whereas those who are capable of killing are already dead.

And since they are dead, I cannot hate them or regard them as enemies.

They don't know what they are doing.

However, I'd like my unjust death to arouse them to life.

To die, while refusing to renounce the desire to life, is to live forever, whereas to live without having discovered the ultimate dimensions of life and without respecting life in others, is in reality the saddest form of death.

Lord, may I love life even in death!

The Judge

Lord,

it's not easy for a judge to pray to you, for you have said: "Judge
    not, that you may not be judged."

We judges don't find it easy to pray because we are also aware
    that our profession bears the curse of having condemned to
    death you, the most innocent defendant in all history.

We cannot forget the words of St. Peter, who said that whoever
    refuses to judge others mercifully will himself be judged
    with justice.

If this holds good for everybody, it is especially true about us,
    who are judges by profession.

But what does judging with justice mean?

Lord, our gravest problem of conscience comes from the fact
    that society has identified justice with the law.

Thus judging with justice no longer means judging with mercy.

But the worst thing is that it is difficult for us to judge even with
    justice.

Justice means giving every one what belongs to him.

But in practice it often comes down to finding in favor of
    whoever is strongest, whoever upholds the system best, the
    one with the most influence.

Those in power made the law to protect themselves.

And justice is restricted to defending this, the law of those in power.

Thus we judges are obliged to condemn those who, in the very cause of justice, are trying to open up new vistas of freedom for mankind.

We have to condemn them because they act against the law as constituted by those in power.

If law is the same as justice, then those who dispute the law, which defends only those in power, will fall irredeemably into the clutches of justice.

Unfortunately, the law was created to defend institutions and not the person.

And so, anyone who says: "Yes, sir!", who obeys the boss, is safe within the law.

Do you see, Lord, how sharp a judge's crisis of conscience may be, precisely because he cannot make use of the most sacred instrument of judgment, his conscience?

We judges can never judge according to our consciences but must go according to the law.

Thus it was that Pilate couldn't condemn you according to his conscience, which told him: "I find no cause in this just man!"

But those in power kept shouting at him: "We have a law, and according to that law, he must die!", the same law for all, whereas in reality, every human being is a mystery, unique in himself.

Often, Lord, we have to condemn people although we are convinced that our sentence serves only as "vengeance" and not as "reform."

We find ourselves in the appalling situation of having to condemn someone according to a law of which perhaps we do not approve and will never approve.

Basically this is like judging against our consciences, although the law officially tries to soothe our qualms.

But, even worse than that, often we cannot apply the law
serenely and justly because we must withstand the pressures
of influential people who besiege us on all sides and want
us to make a mockery of the law for the benefit of their
friends or their interests.

And here I must ask forgiveness in the name of many of us who,
in the exercise of our profession, betray our office by giving
unjust verdicts in favor of such influential people for the
sake of money, because of ambition or out of cowardice.

Lord, I understand that a judge ought to be the freest of men
and the one most prepared at any moment to risk
everything, beginning with his seat on the bench, out of
love for truth.

If the people can't get justice, what remains to them?

Nevertheless, even though we may be full of good will, it's not
always easy for us to see that justice is done.

And why?

Because we are often obliged to judge falsely, without our
knowledge or will.

For, if we are to judge rightly, we need the cooperation of others.

But, for instance, who tells the truth today, especially in court?

Who is able, or even wants, to break through the conspiracy of
organized crime of all kinds which threatens real justice?

What can we judges do against those who hide the truth, who
give perjured witness, or who are totally without scruples?

What are we to do when we find ourselves obliged to condemn
the weak while the real culprits—and we know very well
who they are—will never be judged because they will never
even be brought into court?

Today, Lord, people are discussing the "function" of us judges
and even the need for our existence.

Yes, some are asking themselves if there should be such things
as judges at all.

They are asking if the communities themselves should not be

the ones to delegate their own representatives to judge cases.

They are asking if justice should not be exercised by the citizens themselves, no matter what their background, and not by specialists imposed from above and with the narrow outlook of the law.

They are asking, for example, who is better suited to judge the case of a mother who, in a fit of madness, kills her own child—a group of mothers, or a professional judge?

In fact, Solomon used a somewhat similar method to reach his verdict in the case of the two mothers claiming the same child: he did not judge according to any law but made an appeal to the real mother's love for her child.

If all men are judges, by nature, by conscience or by creation, what is the use of having professional judges?

You have warned us that we shall all be measured by the same measure that we have meted out to others.

And our mercy should increase according as we become, to our sorrow, more aware with every passing day of the enormous margin of error in our judgments.

In this regard, it should be enough for us to remember our monumental injustice in having condemned to death you who are the Author of justice, truth and sanctity.

Lord, what can I ask you for when you will one day judge me as I now judge others?

I suppose the best thing I can do is tell you of my sorrow and my hope.

My sorrow is that I have to judge other men.

My hope and my dream is this: although the law is necessary in an immature society, and although judges will always be needed as long as one man's freedom is not the same as another's, I believe that I can legitimately hope that the day will come when men will finally succeed in so respecting each other's dignity that everyone will feel responsible for the fundamental rights of everyone else, so that we judges will be able to retire in peace because there will be no more cases for us to try.

But I know, Lord, that my dream will never come true because, unfortunately, this society of technicians and bureaucrats has made it more impossible for us judges than for anyone else to dream of a future Garden of Eden.

The Artist

Christ,
I am an artist.

It matters little whether I am a painter, a poet, a sculptor, an
    actor, a musician or a movie director,
    because we're all tarred with the same brush, and
    everybody looks at us with a certain suspicion.

For a start, we seem to be rather atheistic.

But why is this?

Is it because we don't believe in you, or because our sensitivity
    enables us to see more clearly than others through the skin-
    deep religiosity of so many so-called Christians?

It's true that we often find it hard to fit into a sociological,
    institutionalized religion which seems to present no
    difficulty to other people.

Yet we appreciate the most profound values of your faith and,
    perhaps more than most, we see the validity of man's values
    and problems, his creativity, love, his thirst for the infinite,
    and the dynamism that urges us on to create, because there
    is a voice within us which tells us that there is always a
    world, a gesture, a flower, a color, a sound, a face, a feeling,
    something ever new that is still to be discovered.

We artists ought to be able to give a new name to you, the great
    Artist of the universe, since many of the names you have

been given are too commonplace; they are either stale or insipid.

We would like to create a name for you, because we do not reject you but cannot accept the imitations of you presented by those who probably don't have sufficient sensibility to distinguish an original from a shoddy imitation.

We artists ought to ask ourselves why you, who are Art itself, do not always draw our interest, our hearts or our imagination.

If we who have art in our blood knew you as you really are, endless Creativity, we could not possibly remain indifferent to you.

I'm not talking about the bureaucrats of art, who are as insensitive to the truth as are the bureaucrats of religion.

I'm speaking, rather, of real artists.

It doesn't matter whether they are great or insignificant.

It's sufficient that they be genuine artists, that they never be contented with things as they are, that they believe that things can be always new, because you have touched man's flesh with the divine.

It's true, Lord, that we are regarded with something more than suspicion by the professional purveyors of truth, the supporters of the establishment, those who want to keep the *status quo*.

We are critics by vocation.

Art can never be conformist, but is, paradoxically, iconoclastic, "image-breaking," because it flourishes only in a world of freedom and newness.

For us artists, there is no Sabbath, no dogmas, no codes of law, no ready-cooked mush for the mind, nor is there anything sacred.

For us, there is only life, with all its magic and drama, only what's real, only man as he is and as he would wish to be, only a world that is born and dies at every moment, and we cannot feel that we are strangers to, or far from, this birth, because it reflects ever more clearly the true face of a man.

For us, there also exists—and this is why we are not atheists—that which we cannot touch with our hands, or hear with our ears, or encompass totally with our bodies, or fathom completely with our minds.

We don't know what it's called.

But we are searching for it passionately because we know intuitively that it is

the most lifelike clay for our statues,

the best verse for our poetry,

the truest and most real picture for our cameras,

the most beautiful note for our songs,

the most expressive gesture for our interpretation,

and the purest color for our paintings.

Who knows but that you yourself may be this something which we have not yet succeeded in creating but for which we are always yearning, searching and hoping, every morning and every evening?

You may be that masterpiece we dream of but never accomplish, that work of art that sleeps like a child in the heart and the hope of every real artist, and which gives feeling and expressiveness to every one of his daily triumphs.

It is like an infinite force, without a name and without a face, which urges us continually to create ever more and ever better things.

It's true that, if this is so, you are not the God who is praised, loved and adored by the friends of the *status quo* and of dogmatism, those who are afraid of everything new.

Therefore, Lord, forgive us if every day we give you a new name, a name as new every day as our desire to create.

It's not our vocation to be curators of museums, although the museums have been built to house the works of our fellow artists.

Instead, we feel a need for everything that is alive.

It wasn't the artists who built the museums, but rather those
who do not believe that art is always infinite.

It is paganism, pure idolatry, to think that there is such a thing
as an immortal work of art or an immortal artist.

Only man is immortal because God continues to create new
souls.

We want our works of art to be for men; we want them to live in
the midst of life, in the streets, marketplaces, streetcars,
trains, bars, factories, offices, homes and gardens, on the
radio waves and the television screens.

Our works are the art of today for the men of today.

Tomorrow others will come who will speak better and paint
better and sing better for the new man, and who will, in
due course, throw our works into the wastepaper basket if
these works no longer say anything to them.

It's not enough to argue that such-and-such a thing is the work
of a great artist who was admired by his contemporaries.

We must find out whether or not it still says something to the
men of our day.

If it doesn't, then keeping it in an honored place would be like
adoring a false, pagan, dead god.

If a work of art is still alive in itself, it will mean that it had
anticipated time, that it carries within it a breath of eternity,
as do the words of your prophets, which even today can
touch and accuse us because they are still up-to-date.

Therefore, the masterpiece of yesterday that is still alive today
ought to be out among men and not put away in a
museum; it ought to go on proclaiming its message of joy or
registering its protest.

Lord, may we artists succeed in discovering your true face.

We are sure that we shall love you when we see you as you
really are.

And although the world, which calls itself yours, looks pityingly at us poor atheistic artists, may it not reject our message merely because we speak of you in a different, and perhaps not always acceptable, way.

We cannot conceive of a God who has been catalogued and shelved, like a valuable museum piece.

We need to have you alive in the middle of the world.

We need to discover you and to do so through the medium of art, which is our very life.

We know that you have no fixed time for revealing yourself, or one, and only one, place on earth where you may be found.

You are that freedom that reveals itself when and where it pleases.

If you were not, you would not be an artist, nor would you really be "our" God.

The Woman

Lord,
I am a woman.

It's said that only we women know how to pray, perhaps because
praying is the only thing that men let us do with impunity,
especially when we are asking you to give us the patience to
go on acting more or less as their slaves.

I want to pray to you today, but not with the prayer which has
been imposed on us women as the weaker sex.

I want to pray as a person in my own right.

Perhaps we women find it easy to pray to you, Christ, because
you are the only man who defied the mentality and the laws
of your day and accepted women
without prejudice,
without contempt,
without distrust,
without psychological complexes,
and without intolerance.

Many people would have preferred you to have come into the
world without the help of a woman.

But you did not spurn a mother's love.

In a completely natural way, you spoke to women, worked with
them and formed friendships with many of them.

You made the Samaritan woman, who was then living in

adultery, the first missionary of your kingdom.

You weren't ashamed to have the notorious prostitute of Magdala follow you in your apostolate when she chose to accept the true, manly love you freely offered her instead of continuing to sell herself to gratify the self-interested lust of men who were incapable of loving without possessing.

When you had risen from the dead, you did not appear first to the men, but to the women, from whose lips the men had to learn the greatest news in history, the news that you were alive and had conquered death.

As you were climbing the hill to Calvary, it was the women and not the men who wept for you, not out of weakness, however, but because they understood better than anyone else that love and innocence should not be put to death.

You accepted women as persons, but how did other men act?

The men in your own Church, beginning with St. Paul, have always pushed us to one side, mistrusted us, denied us the right to speak and practiced discrimination even in the administration of the sacraments, for they have denied us access to the sacrament of Orders, the priesthood, for which we are more suited by nature than they, since it is a "service."

Perhaps they have excluded us because they have turned the priesthood from being a service to God's people into an instrument of power, caste and privilege, and have not left it as it should be, a free gift of love.

We women are still forced to obey a dogmatic and pastoral theology and a code of canon law written exclusively by men.

Lord, it's said that we talk a lot, but in reality, how often have we women made ourselves heard?

How often have we been allowed to create and use our own language as women?

How often have we been allowed "to do our own thing"?

Is spooning food into the baby the only "thing" we can call our own?

And where is it laid down that men cannot or must not get the dinner ready for their children?

There's a lot of talk today of war between nations, between whites and blacks, between rightists and leftists, but the world is suffering from a wound much deeper than any inflicted by such conflicts, a war that is more widespread, colder and crueller than any other—the war that is being waged between the two halves of the human race, men and women.

Therefore, we women of the twentieth century are changing. We have got tired of being just housewives and have gone out into the factories and offices to earn the money that men value so highly that they say: "You're worth only what you earn!"

Perhaps our rebellion will at times cause us to lose some of our irreplaceable personal values.

We don't deny that the temptation to do so is there, but you must understand, Lord, our sorrow and despair when we see how, for all practical purposes, history has turned us into luxuries for men.

Christ, you are a real man, and we can tell you such things without blushing with shame, because we know that you understand us and are on our side.

We feel that many, if not most, men regard us merely as objects of pleasure and not as persons.

That's why they, in effect, put sentries around us and keep watch over us "to protect us," so they say.

But the fact is that they don't trust us.

Why are men left unguarded and unprotected, but not us?

And then they get angry when we tell them that we feel like slaves!

Lord, what really is a woman's work?

To wash the rice day after day?

To grind the wheat?

To turn the irrigation wheel while her husband sits comfortably smoking his pipe?

I know, Lord, that this doesn't happen literally here but only on other continents.

Yet why is it, Lord, that reading the newspaper, looking at television, going to football games or having a drink with our friends are pastimes that scarcely exist for us women?

And why do we always have to think about getting the supper ready and putting the children to bed after working, not eight, but ten or twelve hours, inside or outside the house?

I know that there are problems, such as these, that we cannot solve by ourselves, problems that have arisen because the whole current of society has been running against us.

But wasn't it the men who, without consulting us, organized, or rather disorganized, society in this way?

According to most men, we were created "for the house," and they were made "for the street," which is the same as saying that we were put on earth to burn ourselves out serving them and waiting up for them!

Yet you brought freedom for us women, too, although we go on being treated like perennial children.

Lord, why is it that, when we get married, we lose even the little bit of freedom we had when we were single?

And why is it that, when men get married, they are often freer than before?

Why is it that, when a woman gets married, she no longer takes any interest in the great problems of the world?

Why does she so often end up by taking refuge in her children and making her whole world revolve around them?

Lord, we don't want to take over completely from the men, nor do we want a world made only by and for women, for that would be as unjust, incomplete and monstrous as the present world of men.

All we want to do is build the world together with men.

We don't join our lives with those of men merely to act as some kind of auxiliary engines to help push them faster toward self-fulfillment.

Rather, we join them in order to live life with them, to fulfill ourselves as persons together with them in everything, and to participate in creativity with them.

Everything else is just slavery and exploitation.

We don't want to replace men in those areas which are more natural to them than to us, nor do we want to be like men in everything, least of all in appearance, because we firmly believe in the sexual differences which you created, Lord.

But we will not accept any differences other than those which arise naturally from the richness of the diversity inherent in men and women.

Therefore, we do not renounce any of our rights as persons.

Freedom has no sex.

It is God's great gift, not to the male alone, but to the human person.

And in the name of this freedom, which belongs to everyone, we want to have a hand in making history, starting with a dialogue between men and women.

We want to be fully persons in everything, as the Creator intended us to be and not as man would have us.

We want to be persons in marriage, which should not be a contract drawn up according to a law which men wrote for themselves, but which should be a free, personal agreement lovingly entered into by two people who then begin to make their own history.

But in reality, what is the role that women often have to play in married love?

How many mothers are there who literally have to sell themselves to their husbands if they are to wheedle money out of them to buy food and clothing for the children?

How many wives are there who, despite illness, indisposition or even disgust, must "satisfy" their husbands if there is to be any peace in the home?

Why don't men have the courage to look for the real reason why so many women are frigid all their married lives?

Or why a wife may prefer to have her husband give her flowers instead of welcoming a complete union of body and soul with him who should be one flesh with her?

What ecclesiastical court has had the bravery to declare that the marriage of a frigid woman is null and void?

Has anyone ever cried out to you her despair when she found that her marriage was not and could never be even remotely like that of Christ and His Church?

Why has the woman's infidelity always been viewed more harshly than the man's?

Lord, I'm sure you're tired of hearing words such as "silence," "obedience," "subjection," "hope of repentance," but always used only in reference to women.

Every time a man feels that he has been rejected by you, as in the Garden of Eden, he tries to put the blame on a woman.

When will our predicament finally be understood?

Yet only when we are allowed to be truly persons will men be able to discover their real selves.

Lord, have mercy on women when, after so many centuries of injustice and slavery, they misuse their most sacred possession, their sexual attraction, to defeat men.

It is our only strength, our only weapon.

It's not that we do not feel the shame and degradation of making ourselves, to some extent, prostitutes for every man we meet.

We do so only because hitherto we have not been able to defend ourselves and make men accept us as persons and look us straight in the eye.

Lord, have mercy also on us because we have not yet plucked up the courage to rebel against being used by men, and have not helped them with our strength to become more men and less pigs.

Help us, Lord, to follow the example of your Mother, the freest and most womanly woman in history, in crying out to the world our own special word for the building up of a new order.

Help us to wake up!

Have mercy, too, on those men who forget too frequently that the world is still on its feet only because, behind each man, there is always hidden the love and hope of a woman who goes on believing in the value of life.

Finally, Lord, please answer two quite indiscreet questions.

In the Garden of Olives, on that night of infinite sorrow, do you think that, if the holy women had been there, they would have fallen asleep, as the Apostles did?

And if it had been a woman, and not Pilate, who had to pronounce the sentence of death on you, do you think you would have died on the cross?

We cannot forget that it was a woman, Pilate's wife, who begged him not to condemn you, but she had no power, only an instinct for justice.

If women had been able to join with men in making
history,
politics,
justice,
and the human community,
it is very likely that certain words, such as "war," would have been erased forever from our dictionaries, because we women know, much better than do men, what pain and death are, because life begins to cry and to laugh in our very flesh.

The Nun

Lord,

I am a nun,

which for many people is the same as saying that I am "childish," "outmoded," "out of touch," "useless," "locked up," "lonely."

Perhaps, however, people aren't far wrong when they criticize a situation in which only a few succeed in being adult, modern, free, useful and happy.

I am one of the many thousands of nuns who today are bearing the weight of an outdated and inhuman structure in which, under the pretext of serving God, they don't even succeed in being persons.

Lord, it is not always the atheists, the Freemasons and the anticlericals who criticize us, as our Superiors sometimes tell us.

Instead, it is often the serious, alert, committed Christians, those who are really trying to live out the teaching of the Gospel, those who suffer when they see the unjust and sometimes intolerable situation of a million women who, in a world that is daily becoming more adult, are obliged to go on being immature and, for the most part, capable of dealing only with children, old people and the sick.

The adult world, the world of youth and the world of labor often despise or pity us, for what do we know about their very real problems, their anxieties, their struggles, their sins, if we are not even allowed to read the newspapers and have to get permission from our Superiors for the smallest things?

Educated in an atmosphere of spiritual privilege, we virgins, the chosen ones, the perfect, the favorites of heaven, must face up to the reality of a world which has values very different from ours, values that we lack:

the freedom to commit ourselves to the liberation of all mankind,

the testimony of poverty and simplicity, not only in person, but also collectively,

the capacity to love everyone without being over-afraid of being contaminated by a world that cannot be as horrible and as diabolical as we think it is, since Christ loved it enough to give His life for it,

the possibility of being able to obey God rather than men, without fear of being reprimanded, and the freedom to retain our originality and not to have to submit to being turned out of a mold,

the possibility of creating a real community with human warmth and with none of the atmosphere of a lodging-house or prison about it,

where the structures and the work we do are designed to help us, who do the work, and the poor and humble, for whom we do it.

In a world in which so much stress is being laid on the part that women have to play in the making of history and in their indispensable integration with men in carrying out the plan of creation and redemption, we nuns are still regarded by many people as the symbols of woman's inferiority.

We live apart from men but, at the same time, we are ruled by men who decide practically everything for us, who always have the last word and who have created for us a form of life that bears the unmistakeable seal of male domination.

Lord, there are about a million of us women who have no
husbands to please but who often find ourselves ordered
about and managed by the sometimes very childish
decisions of men who "know not women."

Lord, don't tell me I'm exaggerating.

It's said that you are our Spouse, but frequently the priests
whom we get as chaplains depict you, if you'll forgive us for
saying so, as a bloodless, effeminate husband.

Christ, the world of today is discovering more and more that you
identify yourself with our neighbor and that you want to be
truly loved in every human being.

Therefore, you don't want people to laugh at or be sorry for us
when they see us chained to a spirituality which would be
unbearable for even the most ruthless ascetic.

Lord, I ask myself in whose name we are forbidden to be
women in the most elementary and innocent things in our
lives.

Certainly not in the name of our commitment to you, since we
did not hand in our resignation as women when we vowed
fidelity to your Gospel.

Your mother never renounced being a woman, and who was
more consecrated than she?

Will people be more free, will they see more clearly the joy of
hope, will you be more present in the world, and will that
world be better and more human, just because we are not
allowed to groom our hair in the most innocent way, or
dress like the normal women of our times, buy a newspaper
or telephone a friend or spend the day with our loved ones?

Only you, Lord, who were a complete man without childish
inhibitions, can understand the state of affairs which, in
your name, forbids us even to be women.

We gave up everything to serve you in our neighbor and
professed publicly before your Church our intention of
doing so.

But now we find ourselves in the terrible situation of appearing before the world as being rich, as being on the side of the rich and as accomplices of the capitalistic system and even as active exponents of exploitation.

Individually, we are poorer than the poorest factory-girl or charwoman, but collectively we belong to a wealthy system.

Personally, I am so poor that I cannot even buy underwear for myself. I have to ask my Superior for every postage stamp I need and for my bus fare. I can't give a coin to a beggar or invite a friend to have a cup of coffee in a restaurant.

I work twelve or fourteen hours a day in a hospital or school. I get no day off, and I haven't even got one hour that I can call my own.

I've lived in a large city for six years, and I've never been downtown.

I never have the pleasure of giving in to an innocent whim or the luxury of a little freedom.

I am like an automaton in the hands of my Superiors.

But the saddest thing is that our bearing witness to you by our self-abnegation in hospitals and schools—which are usually quite grand—loses all its value as witness since it is being paid for by the fees we receive.

In the luxury hotels and expensive hospitals run by laymen, the employees are treated with every consideration by the management, who pass this added expense on to the customer.

But no trade union would allow the abuses we have to endure in the endless hours of work that are heaped on us, not for the glory of God, but to meet the expenses and pay off the debt on the hospital or school.

In fact, if we wanted to spend the same amount of time serving the poor for nothing, we would probably be forbidden to do it because it would be bad for our health.

Lord, one day a Communist remarked to me: "If we had a million unmarried women ready to work for us, we'd have another revolution!"

We are that million women, unmarried and ready to go to work for you, because when we said: "Yes!" to you, we said it unconditionally.

But where is our revolution?

Is it possible that so many of us have so little influence on the world of the oppressed, the enslaved, the unbelievers?

I'm not saying that our work is useless.

We do a lot of things that are beneficial, especially in helping others, but can our activities really be called revolutionary?

When I see so many young women, including some who say that they are atheists, involving themselves so completely in their fellowmen's struggle for freedom, and unafraid of torture or prison, I have to blush with shame for my own sheltered, unadventurous life.

But, Lord, there is something which cannot and will not die in any of us, and that is our irrevocable decision to live completely the essence of your Gospel, overcoming all obstacles to give our loneliest and most abandoned fellowmen our testimony to freedom, resurrection and the serene community search for that bread which increases man's thirst for the infinite.

And this is our hope, a hope which combats our feelings of helplessness to break down the walls of a structure which often kills or frustrates our aspirations to change the world, our desire to open up, honorably but bravely, new roads that will permit us to take our part in our section of history, that desire which burns within us, that irresistible call to be a leaven of liberation in the mass of mankind.

Lord, because of a mistaken fidelity to the past, which no longer exists and which doesn't always deserve approval, we are prevented from freely creating our own world of today as the best guarantee that future generations will not regard us as museum pieces or peculiarly dressed eccentrics who can't even make children laugh.

Lord, sometimes I think that all is lost, and that only by leaping over the wall shall I be able to make my dream of living your Gospel come true.

Sometimes I try to convince myself that one day hope will blossom under my window.

But the winter is dark and cold, long drawn out and exasperating.

It's not enough for us to shorten our dresses while other women are lengthening theirs . . .

We feel that we are betraying you by remaining prisoners of structures which do not reveal you to men.

We have said: "Yes!" to life and freedom, not to passivity or cowardly withdrawal from the world, to unconditional service of our neighbor, who is you, and not to a structure of economic or religious power.

We have vowed fidelity to you, who have called to us from the depths of our consciences, and not to men who think that they have the right to dispose of our lives as they will.

Lord, the only way I can pray to you just now is to cry out my pain, although I shall go on hoping—and praying—that we shall overcome the problems of our structures, for these structures can change or even disappear, while there are a thousand different ways of living this vocation of mine, of being bread of all the hungry, and freedom for all the enslaved, as I live side by side with all those who, like me, have heard the call to this adventure of love for all mankind.

The Single Woman

Christ,
is it true that there is only one form of love?
That only motherhood can fulfill us women?
If a man freely decides to seek self-fulfillment in some way other
    than founding a family, everybody thinks it's quite normal.
The most they will say is that he has preferred to keep his
    freedom.
But if we women choose the same course, everybody smiles
    ironically, and in most cases they think: "The poor girl is
    on the shelf."
Few people believe that we, too, may want to retain our freedom,
    because there is no law of God that requires us to found
    our own families if we want to be persons in the fullest
    sense of the term.
Nor do we have to enter a convent in order to follow up our
    decision to remain single.
Lord, I am a young woman who so far has freely chosen not to
    found a family of my own.
I haven't got time for just one man because I feel that there are
    thousands of people, both men and women, who need my
    encouragement, my companionship as a sister and a friend,
    my time, my freedom and my help.
Lord, I know that many people regard this as sheer idealism.

185

But I'd like to know what their idea of realism is.

I'm quite well aware that all roads can lead to one's fulfillment as a person, and it is precisely for this reason that I am convinced that there is no one sure way to self-fulfillment.

With my own eyes I have seen wives and mothers who are cold, bored, sad and lonely.

I have seen them sigh for a little joy, freedom, and even love.

Lord, is it true that we women can love with all our hearts only the children of our wombs?

Is it true that we can be loved truly only by the man who has chosen us to be his own, exclusive of all other women?

I ask this because I have no children of my own, nor has any man given his whole heart to me, yet I find it difficult to contain all the love that comes to me from all sides, and I haven't got enough time or strength to give a piece of my life to all those who ask me to help them.

And I don't know what sadness, loneliness, boredom or enslavement is.

But I do know what pain is—other people's pain, which I feel as keenly as if it were my own.

Sometimes I am ashamed because I have the feeling that no one has seen as much sun reflected in as many eyes as I; that no one has had so many claims on her affection as I since I opened my heart to everyone and deliberately chose not to love anyone exclusively.

So much so, that I ask myself if I am not destined to love everyone.

Forgive me, Lord, if at times I think I'm incapable of loving anyone because I love everyone, or if it is really others who, by loving someone exclusively, reject everyone else.

Would you like to know my deepest sorrow?

It is not having as many hearts as there are people so that I could give one to each, and no one would be jealous or feel less loved; or not being able to tear out my heart and show everyone that love is infinite and takes nothing from anyone.

I'd like to be able to tell girls like myself that it is possible to fulfill oneself in this way also, and that we have a perfect right to choose as we will; that, since fulfilling oneself means being a person, and being a person means reaching maturity in love, then there are no "only" ways to take our part in history or to share with everyone the love that is coursing through our veins; that the most complete and deepest happiness is to be found in love for everyone and not in the exclusive and possessive love of one man, as the old selfish traditions would have it.

But this love for everyone should be real.

It should extend as far as our total capacity and ability for giving can reach, and it should give all without demanding anything.

It should not be a misguided substitute for love of you, Lord, which would end up by being love for no one.

Nor should it be a love of you which finally becomes more possessive, exclusive and selfish than that of any traditional husband.

Rather, it should be a love that really allows me to love everyone who needs me and who reveals to me his thirst for truly human and divine self-fulfillment.

This is the love I asked you for when I prayed tearfully in front of the false picture of you which they had drawn for me—remember?:

"Christ,
    don't steal others from me!
They are my lifeblood,
    my hope,
    my suffering.
Don't steal them from me!
They don't reflect anybody:

they are my very self until I beget them to happiness.
You are another person:
   you have your own joy, which you share with me.
You are capable of suffering.
You are able to love me.
But those others who are within me are only able to receive my
   love.
Don't steal them from me!
Don't take them away from me!
Wait, wait!
I shall bring them forth to happiness when the time for fear has
   passed."

Christ, break the last chains that have kept poor human
   motherhood so impoverished.
Christ, reveal again to the world, including us women, that there
   is no true human or divine fulfillment unless one launches
   oneself on to the open sea of love.
Christ, tell us once more that love breathes where and when it
   wills and that it follows no set routes, because you are
   infinite Creativeness and have given us the possibility of
   making our own ways.

The Married Couple

Lord,
the two of us are praying to you together now although it is hard for us
to do so.
We are sorely tempted to pray singly, as we usually do.
But then what would our union in marriage mean?
What would be the significance of our having become one
through marriage?
Lord, we have the opportunity to live one of the few moments of
total communion that are possible for man on this earth;
and we know that man's ultimate dimension is precisely
this communion.
Then why do we sometimes find it so hard to maintain this
communion?
Is there something wrong in our relationship with each other
which makes it wonderful sometimes but burdensome at
others?
Lord, is this perhaps because we still regard ourselves as
dependent on each other, or indispensable to each other?
Or is it perhaps because we are not yet completely independent
and are not able to see each other as you see us, not in
relation to you but to ourselves, our own completeness?
Or is it perhaps because we do not really love ourselves?
Lord, I believe that the only way to know love in all its aspects is

to live the marriage relationship in the same way as we live
the total, unlimited personal relationship which you have
with us; or even more, as a relationship which urges us on
towards the infinite.

But is this possible for us humans?

Lord, I know that everything that is possible for you is also
possible for us.

But how are we to begin?

Remember, Lord, that we are burdened with the tradition of the
past, according to which the marriage bond was contracted
solely for convenience, pleasure or children.

And remember, too, that the wife used to call her husband her
lord and master, and that the man used to regard his wife
as a household chattel.

For the most part, these attitudes have disappeared today, but we
still retain some relics of this inhuman outlook which make
it difficult for us to enter into a marriage relationship that is
truly loving and fully respectful of each other as persons.

When I venture to look deeply into the eyes of the one I love, I
really feel that there are no longer any barriers between us;
and both of us know that we are entering the dimension of
the man-God, and that this is the most beautiful and most
natural thing we can do.

We feel that we were born for this.

But, Lord, why are we still not able to possess completely these
discoveries that we have made?

Is it because not all men have yet made these discoveries?

Or is it because we are not accustomed to love and still believe
that it is the privilege of a few fortunate people and not
something that is a normal part of life?

We often justify our incapacity for personal love by saying that
we have to work or have commitments to our children.

But is this true?

Would it not perhaps be truer to say that we are continually

looking for excuses to avoid taking the risk of loving each
   other fully, which is the real object of our existence since
   we decided to join our lives for this very purpose?
Lord, why do we contradict ourselves and not act as we should,
   for reasons that we know are always silly and anti-human?
Why do we continue to believe that the most important thing is
   to have children and to bring them up well?
If we don't have that life which only love can give us, what shall
   we have to give our children?
When we have filled them to capacity with food and culture,
   will they inevitably be happy?
Why are we so slow to understand that, where there is love,
   there is everything, and everything makes sense, but that,
   where there is no love, there is nothing but eagerness to
   escape the boredom of each day?

We ask you, Lord, to help us to understand that looking deeply
   into each other's eyes is not merely that, but is really a
   search for a meeting point between a man and a woman
   who want to begin living a real life, to work together to
   make all things new, and to become like you.
This is so because, if it is true that you have made us in your
   own image and likeness and have been pleased with the
   work of your hands, it is also true that, if we find each other
   and look deeply into each other's heart, we can say that
   God is like us.
And then we shall finally succeed in loving in the same way as
   you do, when you cause your love for all of us to blossom
   from your communion with the Father.
For when love is true and is accomplished in us, it has no
   ending.
It involves all relationships, all other things, and leads finally to
   a full communion and encounter with everything.
Not only does it bring us to acknowledge intellectually that the
   community of man is a vital need, but it also enables us to

live that community in anticipation and to build it up with our love, from which we can always draw new resources so that those who do not yet have a clear perspective of the aim of love, because they have not yet truly encountered each other, may also know it.

Lord, make us see clearly that the ability which we have to build up the human community—that community which is a necessary condition for peace, justice and happiness—is still scant because we may perhaps never have had a total encounter with each other.

Lord, why has married life been for so long a wall to keep others out? And why has it also been directly opposed to the growth of the community?

We two, who are praying to you together, still don't know where we are going or what we shall accomplish. All we know, Lord, is that love for others is the very life of our mutual encounter. And we would like to make our friends, too, understand the value of the human body, of sex, that strange power that has been so stressed and made mythical by the cultures and customs of all times.

How shall we communicate to others in all simplicity the beautiful yet difficult discovery that we have made, that sex, like the body, is the natural domain in which this conjugal encounter can be lived physically? How can we make them understand that it is precisely in sex, experienced in total love, that everything material is redeemed through your person, as a mighty summoning of everything to existence?

Lord, mindful of your words at the dawn of creation, we wish that, when men see all these things, they, too, will understand that they are good, every one of them.

Those Who
Want to Get Married

SHE:

Lord, I am looking for someone to love.

I want to meet a man to whom I can say: "I love you because you acknowledge my right to be myself, as we build a new life together and show others the true meaning of life."

HE:

Lord, I am looking for someone to love.

I want to meet a woman to whom I can say: "I love you because you don't ask me to be 'yours,' but rather to live in marriage with you in the midst of the world, as we discover together everything that exists."

My Own Prayer

Lord, I, too, would like to say a prayer to you, a prayer that contains
only one word—"others."
This is not sheer generosity;
I need others if I am to live.
Without them, I am dead,
I am a dream,
a shadow,
nothing.
They show me my own reality.
They are my God, and they are myself.
Among those others, Lord, there are those who are asleep, who
are in despair, who are hungry, who are enslaved, and
whom I want to awaken, encourage, feed and set free.
And there are those who thirst for justice and have faith in
humanity, by whose side I wish to walk in friendly silence,
asking no questions . . .
These are my traveling companions, and they dream of reaching
the same shore as I, although not all of them call it by the
same name.
But we speak the same language, the language of freedom for all
men.
If, in addition, there are some among them who already have
the light of the resurrection in their eyes, I shall eat the first

fruits of life with them;
and dawn and darkness,
sunshine and snowstorm,
shall be the same for us,
and common bread will be a eucharist.

We shall truly be you.

But, Lord, have I done all I could to ensure that this is what I need and what I want?

Every day I assume the responsibility of finding more ways to do more things; but I would like to give others the chance to ask me what they'd like me to do to help them free themselves.

Lord, I hope that I shall never lack the courage to keep my door always wide open to every human need that serves to fulfill men.

I understand that only thus will my hope of fulfillment have any meaning, and that only thus shall I be able to ask you for fulfillment without blushing for shame.